D1165908

Guns and Suicide

Guns and Suicide

An American Epidemic

MICHAEL D. ANESTIS, PhD

OXFORD
UNIVERSITY PRESS

Oxford University Press is a department of the University of Oxford. It furthers
the University's objective of excellence in research, scholarship, and education
by publishing worldwide. Oxford is a registered trade mark of Oxford University
Press in the UK and certain other countries.

Published in the United States of America by Oxford University Press
198 Madison Avenue, New York, NY 10016, United States of America.

© Oxford University Press 2018

CIP data is on file at the Library of Congress
ISBN 978–0–19–067506–6

9 8 7 6 5 4 3 2 1

Printed by Sheridan Books, Inc., United States of America

Thank you to Joye, my partner in life and brilliant colleague.
Thank you to Jonah and Mary, who leave me awestruck daily.
Thank you to Thomas Joiner, who continues to teach me well
beyond graduation.
Thank you to my family for limitless and unconditional support.
Thank you to my students for shaping my thinking and for the
work you will do in the coming years.

Contents

Introduction

I have spent most of my life living in the northeastern United States, where gun ownership is far less common than in other areas of the country. I grew up among liberal friends and generally came to view guns as the dangerous tools of criminals and as something the world would be better off without. I was exposed to guns so rarely as a child that the encounters I had with them stand out clearly in my memory. As a young boy—likely seven or eight years old—I remember visiting a friend's house one afternoon after school. Our hometown was in a heavily forested area, and my friends and I often spent our time in the woods. During this particular visit, my friend was eager to show me something but also eager to make sure that his parents did not know what we were doing. We told his mother we were going to play outside, which she was happy to hear, and we went on our way. After wandering for ten minutes or so, we came to a spot with high grass, and he pointed to an overturned plastic bucket on the ground. We walked over, and my friend lifted the bucket to reveal a handgun.

I had never seen a gun up close before and was immediately nervous, knowing I was not supposed to be in this situation. My friend picked it up—he was careful not to point it at me or to pull the trigger—but I refused to hold it. I was scared of the gun and felt the fear of the situation much more strongly than the thrill experienced by my friend. We stayed there looking at the gun for probably ten or fifteen minutes and then left, never speaking about the incident again. The sense of danger was so visceral to me—an experience that I now realize is vastly different from that of children raised in different environments. When I think about that day now, the fear is no longer there—although I sometimes imagine my own children in a similar situation and worry about them or their friends being less careful—and I cannot help but wonder what potentially tragic story led to or resulted from that weapon being stored under a bucket in a field.

My sense of discomfort with guns has eased somewhat as an adult. I work frequently with the military and understand the importance of firearms to national security in certain situations. Even still, when I became an assistant professor and moved to southern Mississippi, I was startled by how ubiquitous guns are in day-to-day life and how prevalent they are in the local culture. A year or so after we moved here, I remember walking out of a grocery store with my son—then three years old—and seeing him pause and stare at the automatic sliding door. I assumed he was just interested in how the door could open without us pushing any buttons, but instead he turned to me and asked, "Why is there is picture of a gun in a red circle on the door?" The sign, of course, was there to let customers know that firearms were not allowed inside the store. This is not true for all businesses here and, as such, signs are necessary when an establishment does not allow guns. I had a hard time answering my son's question, but told him that this was a rule because the people in the grocery store felt that it would be safer for gunowners to leave their firearms at home so nobody accidentally gets hurt. I did not want him to be frightened by the thought that anyone around him might have a gun and use it to hurt him or somebody else on purpose, and I also wanted to be careful about how I explained the situation in public, not knowing who else might be listening. At times I find myself standing outside of cultural norms in my hometown, and it leaves me guarded in how I approach certain topics in mixed company.

Guns are on my mind every day now. I am the director of the Suicide and Emotion Dysregulation Lab at the University of Southern Mississippi and generally describe myself as a suicide researcher. Over the past couple of years, my work has increasingly focused on the role of firearms in suicide and steps that could be taken at the individual, state, and national levels to address what has become an increasingly devastating problem in our country. I have addressed this through research, talks at various universities and health-care settings, editorials in newspapers, and in several other venues. Through all of that work, I have become extremely familiar with the data on this topic. The evidence is clear: guns play an important role in suicide. But this knowledge is not widespread, and proper steps to rectify the issue have not been broadly implemented. My goal with this book is to help increase awareness of this problem so as to facilitate progress in resolving it.

I do not anticipate that this book will fundamentally change the reader's opinion about guns and their place in American society: this is not my intention. I will not champion the idea that guns are fundamentally bad any more than I will the idea that they are a daily necessity. It is likely that each reader already has strong opinions on the issues this book discusses, and altering such strongly held convictions is no small matter. Changing your opinions, however, is not necessary for me to accomplish my goal, which is to help more people better understand the connection between guns and suicide and how we can reduce the U.S. suicide rate by changing how people access and store personal firearms. Any talk of gun violence and gun policy should include an accurate and open discussion of the most common form of gun death, which is suicide, and I intend for this book to facilitate informed conversation on this very point. I am a scientist, not a politician, and my hope is that by approaching this issue from a scientific perspective, I can assist in moving us all closer to what should be a bipartisan, unified goal of suicide prevention, regardless of one's stance on the Second Amendment.

To some extent, a comprehensive scientific discussion of gun violence in the United States is impossible because in 1996 the National Rifle Association successfully lobbied Congress to prevent the Centers for Disease Control and Injury Prevention (CDC) from funding research on gun violence. This has resulted in researchers trying to find alternative funding, or conducting their research on this issue without the kind of money that makes high-quality research more plausible. My own funding on this issue, for instance, has come from the Department of Defense through a program known as the Military Suicide Research Consortium. Efforts to cut off funding for gun violence research suggest that the application of scientific inquiry to the topic of gun violence is an inherently political exercise intent on diminishing the rights of American citizens, which is wildly inconsistent with our approach as a nation to other public health issues related to the safety of privately owned items (e.g., cars). As a result, most conversations on gun violence become immediately politicized, and the extant data on its potential causes and solutions is undermined or ignored. I aim to avoid all such politicization. I will certainly present my opinions at times, but I will always distinguish between the data I analyze and my own views.

Our national discussion on gun violence is not only an emotional one but also a remarkably broad one, with a range of sub-issues that extends beyond the question of whether gun ownership should be an unalienable right. For instance, the debate often coheres around the types of guns and ammunition that should be available; some have questioned whether individuals should be able to own assault rifles, high-capacity magazines, and armor-piercing bullets, while others have called into question how we should even define these items. What is perhaps most remarkable about the ongoing discussion regarding guns is the strength of the beliefs on each side of such a wide divide. There appears to be minimal flexibility and a near absence of middle ground. The argument does not center on small disagreements within a larger framework of shared principles but rather on strongly held convictions on points that are mutually incompatible. One side proposes that more "good guys with guns" is the only path to the reduction of gun violence, while the other declares that only the absence of guns will prove a viable solution. One side proposes that any restriction on who owns a gun represents the first step on a slippery slope toward fascism. Indeed, this point is demonstrated quite clearly in the refusal among some politicians and gun rights activists to acknowledge the potential utility of restricting gun access to suspected terrorists on the no-fly list. The other side strongly advocates for universal background checks that extend to all private sales and gun shows.

Like many of the most emotionally charged national conversations at this moment in U.S. history, this discussion can be seen as a confrontation between those who believe government is a problem and that its influence over "personal" matters should be limited and those who think government is a tool with which to enact effective change. Alternatively, the debate could be linked to reactions to national shifts in culture and demographics, with gun rights activists seeking to maintain what they see as part of their individual and national identity; others view a shift away from gun ownership as a key component of an evolving society. Framing such a complicated and fraught issue in any one such manner seems unlikely to make a dent in gun violence rates, however, and the purpose of this book is not to consider the relationship between the United States and guns from the perspective of a political scientist but rather to draw from empirical data to point out a stunning—and deadly—trend.

Suicide is the tenth leading cause of death in the United States. There were nearly 45,000 suicide deaths in this country in 2015. Suicide is substantially more common than homicide and has been for years; indeed, suicide occurs nearly twice as often as homicide. But most people are unaware of these startling facts. They seem even less aware of the fact that the majority of gun deaths in the United States each year are suicide deaths. Despite all of this, suicide is almost entirely ignored within the discussion of guns in the United States. Most popular media stories and sound bites from politicians on the topic of guns are restricted to homicides or accidental deaths (an even more infrequent occurrence, in part for reasons I will discuss in detail later), without even a brief mention of suicide. The exclusion of suicide from the conversation on gun violence is so absolute that some gun rights advocates have argued vehemently that it is actually disingenuous to include suicide deaths in national gun death statistics[1]. It was the absence of suicide from the national conversation on gun violence that prompted me to use the word "epidemic" in the title of this book. I realize some members of the suicide prevention community will view that term as sensationalistic, but I view it as accurate and believe that the data supports my contention. This is an alarming situation that calls for strong and accurate language capable of appropriately framing the conversation. Importantly, epidemics can be reversed but only if the problem is understood and proper prevention strategies are implemented.

With the national suicide rate climbing annually, I would argue that continuing to ignore suicide when discussing guns is costing thousands of American lives every year. This book will thus address guns and suicide in the United States in two parts. In the first section I will introduce the problem, outlining the frequency with which guns are involved in suicide, correcting several important misunderstandings regarding suicide, and building upon that foundation of facts to explain why guns are such an important component of any conversation on suicide. The section will then conclude with a discussion of how suicide deaths by firearms represent a "gun problem" rather than a "mental health" problem. This last point will lead into the second section of the book, in which I explore potential solutions. Much of this section will be centered on empirical support of various gun safety measures in the prevention of suicide.

One of the most bizarre things about being an academic is the realization that many of us spend our careers conducting research on topics we believe to be incredibly important—and then writing about our work in ways that are dense, boring, and overcomplicated. From there, we publish or speak about our discoveries in venues that reach only those individuals who already share our viewpoints. We conduct our studies and analyze the data, and the results appear in scientific journals hidden behind paywalls, or they are presented at conferences attended only by other scientists who would have likely read the paper in journal format anyway. It is almost as though we plan boring parties, refuse to send out any invitations, and then wonder why nobody shows up.

As a whole, academics tend to have both an antipathy toward and ineptitude for communicating their ideas to people who (a) exist outside their field and (b) might not immediately fawn over their work. Perhaps not surprisingly, the results of scientific studies thus do not guide the thinking of people on topics of public interest, which means much of the discussion in the public—and even among policymakers and those in a position to impact how and if we help people on particular issues—ends up focusing on personal philosophies and individual anecdotes. Part of the way through graduate school, my wife and I tried to break out of this pattern by starting a blog—Psychotherapy Brown Bag—in which we took turns writing about scientific studies in a style that we hoped might reach a much broader audience. Although certainly not a website with global influence, the project allowed us a chance to sharpen our skills around speaking about science without relying on esoteric language that loses the reader's attention. That project slowed to a halt as we became professionals and parents, but the years of hard work we put into the blog helped us to develop a better sense of how to distill complex and sometimes esoteric information into a format that holds interest, simplifies without talking down to the reader, and makes clear why work conducted in a lab—an environment that seems so far removed from the day-to-day suffering of people with mental illnesses—actually plays a vital role in helping those individuals recover and take back their lives.

This book will try and build on that experience. And using clearly presented high-quality scientific data to make an unemotional case regarding the role of guns in suicide (and what can be done to prevent people from dying prematurely), I hope to convey my points in a way that reaches out to individuals with varying perspectives on gun ownership and suicide prevention. If you arrived at this book with a strong dislike of guns, I suspect my job will be easy and that, if anything, you will be frustrated that I am not being more critical. However, if you arrived at this book with a strong belief in the fundamental right to own a gun and the danger of any restriction on that right, I suspect the task I've laid out for myself will be more difficult, and I hope that my effort to step out of the echo chamber of academia will help to bridge the gap between us. I promise that gap is not nearly as wide as it may seem. This is not a gun control book but rather a suicide control book, and any such book requires a prominent and honest discussion about guns.

Part I
The Problem

The Demographics of Firearm Suicide in America

S UICIDE IS AN EVENT THAT FOREVER MARKS THE LIVES OF many, creating a pivot point that divides life into "before it happened" and "after it happened." This is obviously true for those who die by suicide, but it also represents the experience of many who lose a friend or loved one to suicide. In some cases, the death is something that loved ones feared might occur for a long time prior to the tragedy. Perhaps the individual had a long history of struggle with mental illness or of several previous non-lethal suicide attempts. Or perhaps he had recently found himself feeling trapped in a difficult and unacceptable situation.

For others, though, the experience is altogether different. In those cases, it is not uncommon for even those closest to the deceased to say, "I never saw this coming." Although I will explain in much more detail later why suicide does not actually come out of nowhere, the fact remains that many of those who die by suicide suffer in silence while seeming to others as though they are fine—perhaps even thriving—and so their deaths are experienced as sudden, shocking, inexplicable, and traumatic by those left behind.

This book aims to not only help readers understand why the specific method that individuals use in suicide attempts is so important but also to pose solutions that may represent common ground opportunities for groups that often do not share much common ground: gun owners and those who are fervently against gun ownership. I will discuss at length scientific evidence and statistics, but before I do I want to set the stage by relating two brief stories that I think are emblematic of suicide in America. I suspect these stories may be surprising because their main characters are not who many people would expect in a story about suicide. I did not choose surprising examples for shock value, however, but rather to make a point that I believe must be central to any forthcoming effort to reduce the burden of suicide in our society: the stereotype many of us harbor of a "suicidal person" is not typical of the majority of American suicides.

In both of these stories, I have removed all identifying information in an effort to protect the privacy of the individuals who died and that of their families. Sharing a story of suicide is a personal decision, and I do not proclaim ownership over these tragedies. Therefore, I would like to share them in a manner that respects those directly involved. The primary aim of this opening chapter is to establish how common suicide is in America—particularly firearm suicide—and to clarify who is most at risk. In doing so, I want to emphasize that risk often exists where we do not expect it, and I believe these stories support this point.

My first story begins with the final days of a successful psychology professor decades into an illustrious career. I will refer to him as "Charlie." I never knew Charlie all that well, but he was an affable, funny, and successful scientist. His work had brought him international acclaim and a global reputation as a leader in his field. Prominent media outlets covered his work regularly. His lab was overflowing with devoted doctoral students hoping to learn from a man capable of helping them become influential scientists themselves. He had been at his university for the better part of 20 years, even serving as department chair during a particularly tumultuous time for the institution.

On a sunny day in April 2016, Charlie did not show up for a graduate seminar he was scheduled to teach that morning. This was unlike him, and several members of the department at the university where he worked at that time were immediately concerned.

Something simply did not *feel* right. Concerned that he might be in trouble, several members of the department drove across town to his house, which was locked. They managed to get in through a window, and once inside they came upon the tragic scene. Charlie had shot himself in the head and died alone in his shower. Outside the bathroom, he had arranged a series of individual notes for specific individuals, outlining logistical needs and explaining his rationale. A woman was scheduled to clean his home that morning, and he had arranged the scene such that she would find the notes and know not to enter the bathroom. His colleagues arrived before that plan could unfold as he had intended. In his notes, Charlie wrote that he realized the timing of the event—just a few weeks before the end of the semester—would cause hardship logistically but that his effort to hold on until the summer break had become unsustainable.

Many of us in the field are still reeling from Charlie's death and likely will be for a long time. I heard some people say that in retrospect Charlie had seemed almost urgent in his conversations and that this may have been a sign that he was asking for help, but that interpretation seems almost certainly influenced by guilt and an understandable desire to ask what one could have done differently to help Charlie. Others said that he had recently given contact information for his adult son to his department's central office, just in case the university ever needed to reach him about anything. Knowing what we know now, this stands out as alarming. But in the middle of the semester when a seemingly happy and healthy professor provides that type of information, concern is not an immediate response.

Despite the shock it caused, Charlie's tragic death is typical of suicide in America. He was a white male in his mid-sixties. He was a gun owner who lived alone. He was skeptical of mental health research and likely was not motivated to seek out evidence-based care for his suicidal thoughts. Demographically, Charlie perfectly fit the profile of American suicide. Despite extensive planning and preparation for his eventual death, he had the outward appearance of somebody who was happy. Those around him did not underestimate his risk of suicide; rather, the idea that Charlie was at risk for suicide at all did not even occur to anyone in the first place. This is not unusual or unreasonable on the part of those close to Charlie, as suicide risk is particularly difficult to detect until an individual has already died, particularly if he or she is intent on doing so and working hard to keep it a secret. Unfortunately, the inability to predict Charlie's death also aligns well with the profile of American suicide. Suicide certainly affects those who are clearly struggling—people who speak openly about suicidal thoughts and who live in such anguish that others worry about suicide long before it happens. Suicide also affects individuals who are not older adult white males. The problem is that the image most people have of suicidal people is far removed from men such as Charlie. Because of this, my sense is that most Americans have a fundamentally incorrect vision of suicide. They are much more likely to envision depressed young women whose lives are besieged with continuous crises (and who speak openly about their thoughts of suicide) than they are to consider lonely older men who neither show nor speak about their distress but who own guns and will one day decide to use them in a suicide attempt. Charlie's death is much closer to the norm than is the vision that most people have when they think about death by suicide.

What would have happened if Charlie had not had access to his gun when he was feeling suicidal? He would have simply found another way, right? Later, I will dig into the mountain of evidence that contradicts this conclusion.

It is important to remember that the story of suicide is not without hope. Consider the struggles of a Hispanic-caucasian solider in his mid-twenties, less than a year removed from basic training. We will call him "Hector." He had no prior deployments, so his struggles cannot be attributed to the horrors of war. Surprisingly, soldiers early in their careers with no deployment histories are a particularly high-risk group in the military. We tend to assume that military suicide is a natural byproduct of combat, but soldiers who have never been deployed represent a large portion of those who die by suicide, and deployment has exhibited a limited association with suicide. Hector served on the Honor Guard, meaning he was on call to work at military funerals—a different life than many of us imagine when we think of soldiers.

From his youth, Hector was a target for ridicule and judgment. Raised in a community with high standards ("You must be good,"

"You must be perfect") he often felt the pressure of being saddled with unrealistic expectations and a family and peer group that did not shy from openly discussing others' shortcomings. His fear of failure and embarrassment reached into every aspect of his life, even keeping him glued to the wall (well away from the dance floor) during military balls. As uncertain as he was about his own worth, Hector nonetheless found a partner in life and married a woman raised in a similar cultural environment. She harbored similarly powerful self-doubts, frequently berating herself and even openly discussing death—although not necessarily suicide.

Hector had the good fortune to receive evidence-based mental health treatment from a therapist invested in his safety, and during his treatment (and at particularly difficult time for him), it came out that he had previously experienced an episode of intense suicidal thoughts. Around this time, an opportunity came along for Hector to take a vacation with his wife to visit her family. He had his leave approved, but his name was left on the "on call" roster and, shortly before the trip, he received notice that he was needed for a funeral. Either unaware that he could ask to have his name taken off the list because of his approved leave or unwilling to let down Command (his commanding officers), Hector told his wife he needed to remain at home while she traveled. His wife was furious, and her departure for the trip was marked by intense arguments.

Shortly after arriving at her parents' home, Hector's wife had a fight with her father and called Hector in distress. Having seen similar scenes unfold in the past, and feeling frustrated by his position so far removed from his wife and her family, Hector was not particularly supportive on the phone. Upset by this, his wife unleashed verbal abuse fueled by her distress—Hector was a bad person, a bad husband, and so on—all ideas that confirmed his own doubts about himself. Shortly after the call Hector went to their storage closet in their apartment building, where he kept his rifle unloaded but also unlocked. During this process, Hector and his wife began a video phone call, so she was witnessing his crisis firsthand. He took the rifle and ammunition and brought it back to their apartment. Leaning against the wall with the ammunition on the table and the rifle balancing on his shoulder, Hector considered whether to move forward with ending his life, his wife constantly pleading with him to stop. As is so often the case in stories such as this, what stopped Hector was a simple yet powerful gesture. One of his dogs walked up to him and licked his face, an honest expression of love that helped him shake off thoughts of death and see a glimmer of hope. Hector's wife called Command, who came to the apartment, took his weapon, and aided him in securing further assistance.

Hector's wife joined him at his next therapy session, and the primary focus of discussion was a gun safe. He indicated that he wanted one—in fact, he had wanted one for quite some time—but his wife was concerned with the expense. She agreed fairly quickly that the cost—certainly not meaningless but also not exorbitant—was worthwhile. The bigger source of contention was when Hector would be allowed to get his gun back from Command. His wife was struggling to trust him—how could she know he would not simply try again?—and her lack of trust was triggering his own doubts about himself. They worked out a plan in which she would trust him to keep himself safe, but she would also be able to change the combination lock on the safe during any future suicidal crisis.

In therapy Hector said that he never considered using any method to end his life other than shooting himself. Suicide had been his goal—not suicide by gun—and yet suicide in his mind took only one form: a self-inflicted gunshot wound. Given this, there is good reason to believe that limiting access to his gun during a crisis might have represented the single most important tool in keeping Hector alive. Fortunately for him and his wife, that is exactly what happened.

Accounts such as these of individuals in crisis—whether they die or survive their attempts—can be powerful tools in humanizing the experience of suicide for those who have not encountered it themselves, but they provide little information in terms of the magnitude of the problem at a population level. As such I think it is vital to accompany individual stories of suicide with facts about how often suicide occurs relative to other causes of death and which individuals are most vulnerable to death by suicide.

To get a full sense of the scope of suicide in the United States, I want to first call your attention to the frequency of suicidal ideation (thoughts about suicide), suicide plans, and non-fatal suicide attempts. In a report developed by Alex Crosby and others for the CDC[1], the authors found that approximately 3.7% of the US population (aged 18 and above) had experienced thoughts of suicide, 1.0% had developed a plan for attempting suicide, and 0.5% had made a suicide attempt in the preceding year. If we apply those percentages to the 2014 US population, this would mean that over 9 million Americans had thoughts of suicide, approximately 2.5 million Americans had developed a suicide plan, and approximately 1.2 million Americans had made a suicide attempt in that year alone. With a national population of over 245 million, even small percentages translate into surprisingly large numbers, so although outcomes such as suicidal ideation and suicide attempts are rare, they nonetheless impact a great many people. People experiencing these thoughts or behaviors and those who care about them may feel isolated and alone in their struggles, but these numbers show that they are not at all alone in their distress.

Without question, suicidal thoughts and plans and non-fatal suicide attempts are vital outcomes to consider, but now let us shift focus to the even greater tragedy of death by suicide. Here again, the numbers may surprise you. In 2014 suicide was the tenth leading cause of death in the United States, with 42,773 reported cases. This would translate to one death for every 28 attempts based on the estimates above; this is a point I will return to in later chapters when I discuss how difficult suicide is despite its reputation as "the easy way out." Indeed, as the numbers above make clear, few people who think about suicide make an attempt, and only a small portion of those who make an attempt actually die by suicide.

To put the suicide death total in context, homicide accounted for 15,809 deaths,[2] and motor vehicle accidents accounted for 32,675 deaths[3] in 2014 (see Figure 1.1). Homicide and motor vehicle accidents seem to be spoken of and covered in the media with much greater frequency, but as these numbers clearly show, suicide is a much larger public health concern. Taking this a step further, by some estimates there were a total of 18 terrorism-related deaths in the United States in 2014 and a total of 3,264 terrorism-related US deaths between 1995 and 2014 (with 3,003 in 2001, the year of the 9/11 attacks).[4] The obvious point here is that the extent to which we hear and speak about specific causes of death does not reflect the actual frequency with which people die by such means. Indeed, if we assumed the number of individuals who died by terrorism each year matched the highly unusual total from 2001, it

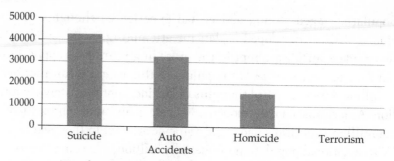

FIGURE 1.1 Deaths (2014).

Source: compiled from http://webappa.cdc.gov/cgi-bin/broker.exe
and http://www.nhtsa.gov/About+NHTSA/Press+Releases/2015/
2014-traffic-deaths-drop-but-2015-trending-higher

would take over 14 years for the terrorism death toll to match the
2014 suicide death toll. Similarly, if we assumed the same number
of individuals died by homicide each year as in 2014, it would take
nearly three years for homicide deaths to match the number of
2014 suicide deaths.

As startling as those numbers might be on their own, they do
not reveal anything about the role of firearms in suicide. In 2014
approximately half of all suicide deaths resulted from self-inflicted
gunshot wounds, with a total of 21,334 Americans dying in this
manner. In other words, 5,525 more people died by suicide using
this single method than died by homicide across all methods combined. Getting even more specific, according to a report published
by *Mother Jones*,[5] a total of 18 individuals died in mass shootings
in the United States in 2014. That same report, with data current
through the tragedy in the Pulse nightclub in Orlando in June
2016, counted a total of 668 mass shooting deaths in the United
States dating back to 1982. In other words, if the same number of
individuals who died in mass shootings in the United States from
1982 through June 2016 died this way every year, it would take just
under 32 years of such nightmares to reach a single year's worth of
firearm suicides. It should be noted that other groups provide much
larger estimates of mass shooting deaths, with the difference stemming from the definition of mass shooting. *Mother Jones* focused
on events not connected to specific crimes (e.g., armed robbery)
resulting in the death of four or more individuals. Other reports,
such as those from the Gun Violence Archive, expand the definition

to involve events in which four or more people (not including the shooter) are shot (although not necessarily killed) in the same location. Also worth noting, however, is that even in these broad definitions, the tragic death totals do not compare in magnitude to firearm suicide numbers. For instance, the Gun Violence Archive counted a total of 268 mass shooting deaths in 2014, or 1.3% of the firearm suicide total[6].

I am not pointing out these discrepancies to diminish the importance of homicide deaths in general or mass shootings in particular. Both my status as a father and my position as somebody who works on a college campus leave me sitting up at night worrying about these events rather often. I also grew up a few towns away from Newtown, Connecticut, where the tragedy at the Sandy Hook Elementary School took place, so I feel a personal sense of pain when I think about that particular event. The reason I am citing these numbers is to make clear the fact that even though we almost never talk about firearm suicides, they are occurring around us at an alarmingly high rate—far more often than headline-grabbing events that tend to dominate conversation and media attention. Every bit of press coverage that has been devoted to firearm homicide deaths, mass shootings, or otherwise, is justified. The problem is simply that much more frequent and equally tragic firearm suicides receive such little coverage and as such most people do not even consider suicide when discussing gun violence.

Who accounts for the bulk of US suicide deaths each year? And, as I will discuss later, why does this matter? The biggest distinction is between the sexes, with men accounting for 33,133 (77.4%) of the deaths in 2014 (see Table 1.1). This means that for every woman who dies by suicide, between three and four men will die. In terms of race, white people have a suicide rate that towers above that of other ethnicities, with 15.43 per 100,000 having died by suicide in 2014. The next highest rate among groups classified on the CDC website was 10.82 for American Indians/Alaskan Natives, although due to their low population, suicides in this group only accounted for 489 deaths. In terms of age, middle age is currently the group with the greatest risk, with a suicide rate of 19.35 per 100,000. Even these numbers, however, as detailed as they are, only tell part of the story. Combine some of these figures and more startling trends emerge. For instance, for white males aged 66 and above, the suicide rate in 2014 was 27.69

TABLE 1.1 2014 Suicide Deaths

	Total (Number per 100,000)
Total Suicide Deaths	42,773 (13.41)
Sex	
Men	33,113 (21.10)
Women	9,660 (5.97)
Age Groups	
<18	1,344 (1.83)
18–30	8,097 (14.03)
31–45	10,122 (16.34)
46–65	16,013 (19.35)
66+	7,193 (16.78)
Race/Ethnicity	
White	38,675 (15.43)
Black	2,421 (5.46)
American Indian/Alaskan Native	489 (10.82)
Asian	1,188 (6.12)

Source: compiled from the CDC's WISQARS database, available at: http://webappa.cdc.gov/cgi-bin/broker.exe

per 100,000, more than double the national rate. There are many ways we can divide up the population when considering the question of who is most likely to die by suicide: some of these are undoubtedly more useful than others, but certain factors such as race and age (and, as we will see, gun ownership) appear particularly relevant whether considered in isolation or in combination with one another. Recall the stories of Charlie and Hector that I recounted at the beginning of this chapter—these numbers should help clarify why I framed them as representative of suicide in the United States.[7]

It would not be productive to think of suicide only in terms of the groups at greatest risk. Although less common, the death by suicide of a woman, teenager, or racial minority is certainly no less tragic. That being said, I relay these particular statistics because, as our conversation about firearms and suicide develops, these groups (for instance older white males) are going to show up again and again, and that will help us to better understand which individuals are most

TABLE 1.2 2014 Homicide Deaths

	Total (Number per 100,000)
Total Suicide Deaths	15,089 (4.96)
Sex	
Men	12,491 (7.96)
Women	3,318 (2.05)
Age Groups	
<18	1,435 (1.95)
18–30	6,277 (10.88)
31–45	4,283 (6.91)
46–65	2,953 (3.57)
66+	855 (1.99)
Race/Ethnicity	
White	7,362 (2.94)
Black	7,876 (17.78)
American Indian/Alaskan Native	263 (5.82)
Asian	308 (1.59)

Source: compiled from the CDC's WISQARS database, available at: http://webappa.cdc.gov/cgi-bin/broker.exe

likely to die by suicide, why they choose to do so, and what we can do to prevent others from making this same decision in the future.

I always find it helpful to compare trends for one event to those of another in order to better understand what they mean. The obvious comparison here is with homicide. If we examine those same groups, what you will see is that, here again, men are far more likely than women to be victims, accounting for 12,491 (82.7%) homicide deaths in the United States in 2014 (see Table 1.2). Unlike suicide, homicide is most common in a younger age group, with individuals aged 18 to 30 dying at a rate of 10.88 per 100,000. Also unlike suicide, homicide is a far more common factor in deaths of black individuals, with a rate of 17.78 per 100,000 (7,876 total deaths). Indeed, the second highest homicide death rate among racial groups was 5.82 per 100,000 American Indian/Alaskan Natives, but this group only accounted for 263 deaths.

These numbers give us a relatively good sense of *who* dies by suicide, but another important factor to consider is *where* people are most likely to die by suicide. The environments we live in can play an important role in our health in a number ways and can also reflect our vulnerability to other variables that could influence our health (our incomes, for instance). One way scientists consider this notion is by using the variable of population density—the average number of people living within one square mile. Most folks, myself included, think about this on a state level, meaning that we will compare the population density of one state to another (e.g., Connecticut relative to Wyoming), but comparisons can also be done on a more local level if the data is available (cities versus towns, for instance). With suicide, a regular finding—and one that stands in stark contrast to homicide—is that the lower the population density, the higher the suicide rate tends to be. Put more simply, suicide rates tend to be higher in rural areas, whereas homicide rates tend to be higher in urban areas. There are several reasons why suicide may unfold this way, but two that stand out are access to health care and levels of gun ownership. Health-care access tends to be lower in more rural areas whereas gun ownership is most prevalent. This can be seen by looking at a table of state-to-state population density, suicide rates, and percentage of suicides resulting from guns (see Table 1.3).

A quick glance at Table 1.3 reveals a fairly clear picture. In more rural states—those with a lower population density—the overall suicide rate was higher, and a higher percentage of suicides resulted from guns. Although not a perfect pattern, this reflects higher suicide rates in many southern, southwestern, and north-central states. As such, our picture of the prototypical American suicide becomes a bit clearer, with middle-aged or older while males living in rural areas more likely to die by suicide, with guns playing a particularly prominent role in such deaths.

One reasonable critique of numbers such as these is that you can lose the connection to individual stories and the struggles and idiosyncratic life moments that lead a specific person to the point at which he or she decides to attempt suicide. I absolutely acknowledge and understand that, but it is not an either/or proposition. To prevent suicide, we need to understand it both at the micro level and macro level, meaning that we must develop a sense of what individual factors might increase risk (owning a gun, feeling depressed, getting divorced, etc.) as well as what population level factors could increase risk (access to health care, legislation impacting gun ownership or

TABLE 1.3 State to State Population Density, Suicide Rates, and
Percentage of Suicides Resulting from Guns

State	Population Density	Overall Suicide Rate	Firearm Suicide Rate	% Suicides by Gun
Alabama	95.40	14.74	9.88	67.0%
Alaska	1.30	22.67	15.61	68.9%
Arizona	58.30	18.48	10.15	54.9%
Arkansas	56.90	17.36	10.89	62.7%
California	246.10	10.86	4.08	37.6%
Colorado	50.80	20.22	10.06	49.8%
Connecticut	742.60	10.54	3.48	33.0%
District of Columbia	10,588.80	7.89	2.12	26.9%
Delaware	475.10	13.47	6.31	46.8%
Florida	364.60	15.26	7.73	50.7%
Georgia	173.70	12.82	8.32	64.9%
Hawaii	218.60	14.37	2.32	16.1%
Idaho	19.50	19.58	11.14	56.9%
Illinois	232.00	10.85	4.14	38.2%
Iowa	55.30	13.10	6.24	47.6%
Kansas	35.40	15.67	8.20	52.3%
Kentucky	111.30	16.47	10.63	64.5%
Louisiana	107.10	14.60	9.55	65.4%
Maine	43.10	16.54	8.72	52.7%
Maryland	610.80	10.14	4.63	45.7%
Massachusetts	858.00	8.84	1.93	21.8%
Michigan	175.00	13.66	6.77	49.6%
Minnesota	68.10	12.57	5.64	44.9%
Mississippi	63.70	12.69	8.38	66.0%
Missouri	87.90	16.77	9.70	57.8%
Montana	7.00	24.52	14.56	59.4%
Nebraska	24.30	13.34	7.07	53.0%
New Hampshire	147.80	18.62	8.29	44.5%
New Jersey	1,210.10	8.79	2.17	24.7%
New Mexico	17.20	21.53	11.70	54.3%
New York	417.00	8.61	2.40	27.9%
North Carolina	202.60	13.59	7.63	56.1%

(continued)

TABLE 1.3 Continued

State	Population Density	Overall Suicide Rate	Firearm Suicide Rate	% Suicides by Gun
North Dakota	10.50	18.53	11.49	62.0%
Ohio	283.20	12.86	6.42	49.9%
Oklahoma	56.10	18.98	11.22	59.1%
Oregon	40.90	19.70	10.63	54.0%
Pennsylvania	285.50	14.21	7.01	49.3%
Rhode Island	1,017.10	10.71	1.90	17.7%
South Carolina	158.80	15.58	9.91	62.9%
South Dakota	11.10	16.53	8.91	53.9%
Tennessee	157.50	14.47	9.10	62.9%
Texas	101.20	12.07	6.64	55.0%
Utah	35.30	18.99	9.45	49.8%
Vermont	68.00	19.79	9.42	47.6%
Virginia	209.20	13.48	7.51	55.7%
Washington	104.90	15.85	7.80	49.2%
West Virginia	77.10	19.40	11.73	60.5%
Wisconsin	106.00	13.36	6.11	45.7%
Wyoming	6.00	20.54	13.35	65.0%

Source: https://www.cdc.gov/injury/wisqars/fatal.html

storage, employment trends). In doing this, we can get a sense of the many different opportunities available to us for suicide prevention. We can also better understand which variables influence suicide at both the individual and population level, and I will soon present data that makes a compelling case that gun ownership, storage, and safety practices represent such variables.

Myths and Theories of Suicide

S HORTLY BEFORE MY DAUGHTER TURNED TWO, SHE AND I were sitting on the floor in our living room playing. We did not have any distinct game going on. Instead, we were simply stepping in and out of brief interactions with different books, stuffed animals, puzzles, and balls. At one point, she looked up at me, handed me a toy, and said with great conviction: "fix it." I am not particularly mechanical, but I felt confident that I could handle this one. I took the toy—a clunky plastic object meant to resemble a pre-smartphone-era cell phone—and pushed a few buttons. As my daughter's indignant stare had already informed me, the phone was not making any noises or lighting up, and this was making the toy a lot less fun than she fig- ured it should be. "I've got this," I said, and I walked across the room to the drawer where we keep our batteries. I felt good about myself as I used a screwdriver to open the battery casing and my daughter looked on, impressed. Once I completed that task, I walked back over to where she was sitting, pressed a button . . . and nothing happened. "That's okay," I said, and I began trying other solutions. I pushed the same buttons I had pushed before but this time with greater fury. I smacked the top of the toy three or four times. I stared at it silently and bit my lip. None of these things really improved the situation at all, and eventually I handed it back to her and said, "I think this toy just might not be working anymore." As is often the case with my youngest, she took this in stride and seemed ready to move on to the next game. Before doing so, however, she flipped the phone over and pushed the power button. The phone immediately started working. It had been powered off the entire time.

Sometimes, when repeated attempts to solve a problem fail to produce the desired results, it is simply because we did not fully understand the problem in front of us on a basic level. The example of my daughter's toy is obviously a silly one, but it nonetheless makes a point that can be applied seriously to problems that have had much more dire consequences throughout history. Before the development of germ theory, for instance, we did not understand the basic nature of many physical illnesses, and as such we were ill-equipped to prevent and treat such conditions. Without a basic understanding of an obviously important topic, we tend to fill the void with deeply held convictions based on what feels like compelling evidence: strong memories, powerful anecdotes, and personal convictions driven by religious beliefs or other values. When people develop entrenched and misguided views on specific issues, making progress on solutions is difficult. It is my contention that (at least until fairly recently) this has been one of the primary problems in the field of suicide prevention: many people are misinformed about what suicide is, who is most vulnerable, and how individuals come to be at risk for dying by suicide. That lack of understanding has interfered with our ability to prevent suicide, and it has given life to beliefs that should have expired long ago.

Suicide, like most other serious problems, is complicated. In addition to its generally complicated nature, suicide is also an emotional topic for many and highly stigmatized throughout the United States and other cultures. This situation complicates conversations on the topic across a variety of forums. As one poignant example, I have spent the past two years serving as the moderator of the listserv for the American Association for Suicidology (AAS). Although the listserv is not limited to AAS members, subscribers to it match the AAS membership quite well, representing a richly diverse set of professions and experiences. Academics such as myself play a prominent role but so do health-care providers, those who have lost loved ones to suicide, and people who survived a suicide attempt in the past. Indeed, many listserv members could accurately be described by more than one of those labels. The emotional nature of suicide is highlighted here, though, as even on a listserv designed specifically for those invested in suicide prevention to discuss suicide, the topic can be difficult to approach. Quite often, word choice or interpretations of data result in unintentionally hurt feelings and a sense of tension across the listserv community. Consequently, many potentially interesting conversations either stop entirely or derail, turning into arguments over tangential issues and pulling attention away from the primary point of the conversation. Particularly uncomfortable interactions such as this occasionally silence the entire listserv for days, with members presumably hesitant to contribute anything for fear of being misunderstood and getting drawn into a conflict. For example, a discussion of whether or not the vast majority of individuals who die by suicide would qualify for a mental illness diagnosis at the time of their deaths elicited a wide-ranging and emotionally charged argument from individuals with differing perspectives (e.g., attempt survivors, researchers) that quickly stopped being informative and ultimately shut down conversation in the group for days.

Conversations about suicide can grow emotional and uncomfortable quickly and a disagreement about words can prompt individuals to feel disparaged, ultimately complicating efforts for anyone to remain focused on the issue at hand. If those who have an active interest in discussing suicide struggle to do so in a forum designed specifically for that task, imagine how complicated it is to open a broader dialogue on suicide at the national level. If it is this difficult for individuals to discuss the science of suicide prevention within a community of suicidologists, it is fairly absurd to expect that open and accurate discussions of suicide will occur in highly public forums such as political debates and televised news stories.

Because of all of this, a sort of mythology has developed around the topic of suicide, resulting in widely held and seemingly reasonable beliefs about suicide that are, in fact, erroneous. For instance, many believe suicide is often impulsive, that it is cowardly, and that it occurs most frequently around the December holidays. None of these are correct, but plenty of well-educated people—including some whose professional lives are built around suicide prevention— would argue otherwise. Later in this chapter I will provide evidence supporting my contention that these are myths, but first it is worth noting how plentiful, widespread, and entrenched many such beliefs are. The psychologist Thomas Joiner wrote a book on the topic, simply titled *Myths about Suicide*.[1]

A situation like this, with so many individuals developing distorted understandings of important phenomena, could potentially be explained by a failure of a well-validated theoretical understanding of suicide to take hold outside of academic communities. Each spring, I teach our doctoral students in a seminar class devoted entirely to understanding evidence-based treatments for specific mental illnesses. The class largely involves reading published clinical trials and developing an understanding of the strengths and weaknesses in how we study specific treatments. During the first two weeks, however, we spend a good deal of time discussing the work of Sir Karl Popper. I love this portion of the class, although given how dense Popper's work can be, I often get the sense that my enthusiasm is not necessarily shared by all the students. In his classic book, *The Logic of Scientific Discovery*[2], Popper described the importance of developing a clearly articulated theory about how something works, with that theory, to the degree possible, based on a series of previous findings that have set the stage for our current way of thinking. From there, Popper argues that it is vital to develop a series of testable hypotheses—guesses about how specific things relate to one another—and to define ahead of time what "being right" would look like: it is then possible for others to see if you are wrong (and impossible for you to manipulate whatever results appear into supporting your beliefs). In a sentence that has heavily influenced my thinking as a scientist, Popper noted that "no matter how many instances of white swans we may have observed, this does not justify the conclusion that all swans are white" (p. 27). No matter how easily we can recall a steady stream of observations that seem to tell us that a behavior works a certain way, our observations are not equipped to uncover truth. In fact, our own emotions, biases, and limitations of memory often set us up to be wrong, even as we feel certain we are right. Popper saw science as a continuous march toward a complete understanding of the world—a march that would never actually end but would get closer and closer to its destination by rigorously forcing us to take our most strongly held beliefs and put them to the test. Those theories that pass the test live on to be challenged again. Those that fail the test are discarded or revised, and the march continues on.

So our understanding of difficult topics—with suicide being one meaningful example—should be driven by what has actually been found to occur rather than by how we believe it should occur. In his more elegant words, Popper stated

> with the help of other statements, previously accepted, certain singular statements—which we may call 'predictions'—are deduced from the theory; especially predictions that are easily testable or applicable. From among these statements, those are selected which are not derivable from the current theory, and more especially those which the current theory contradicts. Next we seek a decision as regards these (and other) derived statements by comparing them with the results of practical applications and experiments. If this decision is positive, that is, if the singular conclusions turn out to be acceptable, or verified, then the theory has, for the time being, passed its test: we have found no reason to discard it. (p.33)

Popper's point has important implications for a variety of problems, ranging from silly ones such as a toy's failure to light up and make sounds to profound ones such as humanity's struggles to effectively prevent suicide. Theories of suicide have existed for many years, but most of those theories were not put through the vigorous testing proposed by Popper, and even those that took hold in the scientific community largely failed to develop any prominence in the minds of the general public. As such, other ideas, untested and inconsistent with evidence, were left to fill the void and myths about suicide became widespread and accepted as truths.

Recently, the scientific community has made a concerted effort to develop, test, and promote theories of suicide that directly address common myths, and my hope is that they will begin to take hold on a national level so as to promote open and accurate conversations about suicide and to implement theory-driven, effective prevention and treatment strategies. Most relevant to our discussion here, two new theories of suicide—both of which are important in how I think about the topic—provide a clear framework for understanding how and why guns play such an important role in suicide in the United States.

The Interpersonal Theory of Suicide (ITS)

In 2005 Thomas Joiner published *Why People Die by Suicide*,[3] which outlined the interpersonal theory of suicide—his view on how and why suicidal desire emerges and what facilitates a person's transition from thinking about suicide to actually making a suicide attempt. That same year, I moved to Tallahassee, Florida, and began my first year in graduate school, working towards my PhD in the clinical psychology program at Florida State as a member of Dr. Joiner's laboratory. Because of this, I feel rather privileged, as I have had a front row seat and have been able to play a role of sorts in the growth of the ITS: from a theory developed in a lab in Tallahassee into possibly the leading framework worldwide for understanding suicide.

The ITS is a theory that Karl Popper would have loved. It puts forward specific hypotheses about how suicide emerges, exposing itself to the possibility of being refuted. It has also evolved, as the evidence has led Dr. Joiner and others in directions they did not anticipate in 2005. One of the things that I value in this theory is its ability to explain many of the most perplexing statistics I noted in chapter 1. The ITS offers explanations for why women think about suicide far more often than men do, and why men die by suicide far more often than women. It also explains why suicide is unlikely to be impulsive—suddenly occurring to those who moments or hours earlier had not considered it. Perhaps most importantly, the ITS has the ability to forcefully dismiss many of the most hurtful myths about the behavior—that it is a sign of weakness and cowardice or that it is engaged in for selfish reasons. Joiner does not claim that suicide is a laudable behavior, but he clearly explains how, from the perspective of the suicidal mind, suicide looks far different than it does from the perspective of someone who is not suicidal.

Thwarted Belongingness

Joiner's first point is that in order for people to develop serious thoughts of suicide, they must feel hopeless about two specific aspects of their lives: their interpersonal connections and their ability to make valuable contributions to society. Humans are a remarkably social species. In fact, some argue that we are one of the few species on this planet that fit the category of *eusocial*[4], which among other things indicates that we view ourselves as part of a larger community of other people and play specific roles in the continued life of the species. When our connections to others are frayed—whether that means through a divorce, through solitary confinement in prison, through separation from the unit when National Guard personnel return from deployment, or some other social separation—this has pronounced negative consequences for us. Indeed, several theories of depression place social isolation and lower quality of interpersonal relationships as primary causes of that affliction[5,6] and many of our most successful forms of treatment for mental illnesses place a heavy emphasis on increasing the quality of interpersonal connections.[7,8,9]

Joiner notes that social isolation does not always involve rejections from others. Thwarted belongingness—the term for social isolation in the ITS—simply reflects a perception a person has that he or she is lacking strong, reciprocally caring relationships in which he or she feels understood. For some, this means a sense that nobody loves them, but for others, it simply means that although they may be loved, they are perhaps misunderstood, and as such, there is a distance between them. Fortunately, increasing connectivity does not necessarily require fundamentally altering how a person interacts with the world. Indeed, studies have shown that the simple mailing of a letter to former clients by mental health clinics—somewhat personalized but largely from a template—is associated with lower rates of subsequent suicidal behavior.[10] Similarly, there are data showing that when there are big sporting events (e.g., Super Bowl, the Miracle on Ice), the community of individuals who tune into that shared experience benefits, as evidenced by lower suicide rates on the days of such events.[11] For a moment, whether it is due to a celebration or shared distress, we see ourselves as part of a larger group. This ability of individuals to "pull together" over shared experiences speaks to a remarkable opportunity for people to protect themselves from suicidal thoughts. It also may explain why the persistent myth that suicide is most common around the Christmas holidays is off base. Even for those who feel disconnected from people they care about, the holidays can represent a larger event that they are sharing with others. Indeed, although death by suicide certainly occurs at such times, there is some evidence that the rates are lower than average in December, with rates in the United States peaking in the spring.[12] When there is a less obvious connection between the individual and the community, perceived isolation becomes much more plausible and possibly more dangerous. Any death by suicide is a tragedy, but one characteristic that I always find profoundly upsetting is that those who died likely believed that their deaths would cause little or no lasting distress: they erroneously believed their social connections were too thin to have much impact on the world around them.

Perceived Burdensomeness

Thwarted belongingness is an important aspect of how suicidal desire develops in the ITS, but it is not the only one. The second component is what Joiner calls "perceived burdensomeness." The theory proposes that as people develop the belief that they do not make valuable contributions to the world around them, and the sense that others would benefit more from their deaths than from their continued lives, vulnerability to suicidal ideation increases. Just as is the case with thwarted belongingness, the key here is that this is the perception on the part of the suicidal individual and not the reality. Just as those who die by suicide are not unloved, they also are not valueless burdens on the world. They simply feel that way, but the presence of the feeling, at least in this case, may be more important than the truth of the feeling. Feelings of perceived burdensomeness need not stem from specific incidents in someone's life, but examples of events that might cause such feelings include losing a job, returning from deployment and not understanding what the next "mission" is, or doing something that leaves one feeling as though he has let others down.

According to the ITS, in order for serious thoughts of suicide to emerge, a person must experience elevations in both thwarted belongingness and perceived burdensomeness and feel hopeless that these beliefs will change in the future (see Figure 2.1). Statistically,

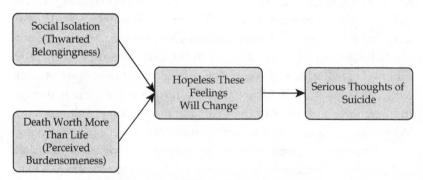

FIGURE 2.1 The Path to Suicidal Thoughts in the Interpersonal Theory of Suicide.

this means that the theory proposes a two-way interaction; in other words, the relationship between one variable (thwarted belonging-ness) and another variable (suicidal ideation) depends upon how much you have of another variable (perceived burdensomeness). So, without question, both thwarted belongingness and perceived bur-densomeness are relevant to suicidal thinking on their own, but that relationship is strongest when a person is experiencing high levels of both variables. Since 2005, a number of studies have tested this idea. Not all have supported that the two-way interaction is necessary, but several have, both in civilian[13] and military[14] populations.

Capability for Suicide

All of this information is helpful in understanding what might drive a person to think about suicide, but what we have discussed so far does not provide any real insight into who will actually move from simply thinking about suicide to making a suicide attempt. As I noted in chapter 1, one of the most important sta-tistics related to suicide (and thus one of the most important sta-tistics for any viable theory of suicide to explain) is that the vast majority of those who think about suicide do not make an attempt and the vast majority of those who make an attempt do not die. Put simply, suicide is difficult. As Joiner noted in *Myths about Suicide*, "It is tragic, fearsome, agonizing, and awful, but it is not easy" (p. 29). For understandable reasons, we are hardwired to sur-vive and to maintain bodily integrity. From a simple evolutionary perspective, this instinct increases the odds that we will pass on our genes to another generation, thereby securing the continued survival of our species. This would explain why, for most of us, when we approach a situation that might cause us harm (or worse, death), a fear response kicks in and we hesitate or take immediate defensive actions. Suicide is in direct contrast to any such instinct, as it requires people to approach death.

I mentioned earlier in this chapter that one particularly common myth is that suicide is an "easy way out." What is startling about the persistence of this myth is that it remains so common among those who spend time learning about suicide. In fact, influential theories of suicide that predate the ITS and were developed within academic cir-cles specifically refer to suicide as an "escape."[15] If this were the case, however, and suicide was a simple way to step away from life's problems in the midst of a difficult moment, the statistics of suicide would look far different. Put another way, if suicide is easy, why do so many people who so desperately want to die never make an attempt, and why do so many who make an attempt survive? Furthermore, why do 90% of those who survive an attempt never die by suicide later in life?[16] If suicide were easy, we should expect that a much higher percentage of those who want it would actively pursue it, even if it took multiple tries. Certainly some people do—those with multiple past suicide attempts are often who we are most worried about in terms of future death by suicide[17]—but they represent exceptions to the rule.

The ITS proposes something vastly different: that most people simply are not capable of dying by suicide. Within this theory, the capability for suicide is conceptualized as having two primary components: an increased fearlessness about death and bodily harm and an elevated tolerance for physiological pain. When Joiner first developed the ITS, he referred to this as the "acquired capability for suicide," noting that individuals would develop this diminished fear response and elevated pain tolerance through repeated exposures to events and experiences that were painful or involved the threat of death. Without question, measures of the capability for suicide have been shown to be associated with increased exposure to such experiences (e.g., combat exposure, repeated instances of non-suicidal self-injury, physical aggression, prior suicide attempts),[18,19] but recent data have also demonstrated that there is a significant genetic component to this capability.[20] So the story now appears to be that the capability can be acquired, but not everyone is born with the same degree of capacity for suicide.

When I have given talks about the idea of the capability for suicide, I have occasionally heard audience members express concern—noting that words such as "capacity" seem to glorify the notion of suicide. This is not my intention. Acknowledging that suicide is difficult does not equate to claiming it is admirable; rather, it simply recognizes that some behaviors run counter to our evolutionary instincts and that overcoming such instincts—for reasons strongly tied to the survival of our species—is not an easy task. A vital point to consider when trying to understand the notion of the capability for suicide is that, in and of itself, it is not a bad thing. The vast majority of those who are capable of suicide have never had thoughts of suicide and will not develop them in the future. Indeed, if we look at measures of capability across studies, a universal finding is that it is completely unrelated to suicidal thoughts. In fact, in many circumstances, the capability—at least as defined by the ITS—could prove beneficial. For a soldier, a minimal fear of death may enable survival in combat. This same variable may enable a firefighter or police officer to approach the most dangerous situations involved in such lifesaving work. For an athlete, an elevated pain tolerance may enable continued training and persistence in an effort to improve and win. For a surgeon, it may mean the ability to make quick decisions and precise movements in gory situations in which a patient's life is at stake. The problem is not the capability—it is the relatively rare pairing of the capability with the desire for suicide.

This last point gets to the primary hypothesis of the ITS and, as I noted earlier, plays an important role in how I think about suicide more broadly and firearm suicides in particular. In the absence of the capability for suicide, suicidal desire—tragic in its own right but not fatal—is unlikely to result in a suicide attempt, or at least a suicide attempt with a high likelihood of lethality. An individual must exhibit both the desire for suicide (intractable beliefs in social isolation and burdensomeness leading to suicidal thoughts) and capability for suicide in order to engage in serious or lethal suicidal behavior (see Figure 2.2). He must want to and be able to approach the potential for pain, dismemberment, discomfort, fear, and death—all things that understandably terrify most of us to such an extent that suicide

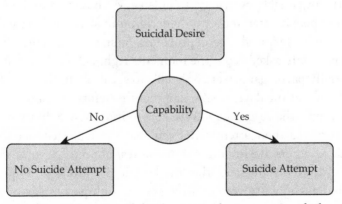

FIGURE 2.2 The Path to Suicidal Behavior in the Interpersonal Theory of Suicide.

is simply not something we are capable of. Thus far, although this main hypothesis has not been universally supported, the data are largely consistent with this notion[21,22].

Is Suicidal Behavior Impulsive?

In the beginning of this chapter, I noted that one prominent myth—both in the general public and in academic circles—is that suicide is frequently an impulsive act. In this line of thinking, individuals who had not considered attempting suicide suddenly do so in response to an unforeseeable upsetting event. Such suicide attempts would be frantic, involving whatever method was closest at hand, driven by the anguish of the moment as much if not more than the distress of all the moments leading up to the attempt. If you close your eyes and imagine somebody in a crisis, this probably is not a particularly difficult scenario to envision. Nothing about it sounds fundamentally unreasonable. Many scientists agree; and, in fact, it is not uncommon to see studies referencing prior results that have shown that many individuals who survive suicide attempts report that they made the decision to try and kill themselves hours or even moments before they ultimately made the attempt.

In 2014 I led a team of researchers skeptical about this conclusion, and we published an article in *Personality and Social Psychology Review*[23] that combined data from decades of relevant studies. Our results—unsurprising to us but in direct contrast to what many are still saying on the topic—did not support the idea that suicide is frequently (or possibly even ever) impulsive. With respect to the studies showing people often report only deciding to attempt shortly before the attempt, we found several problems. First, the researchers for the most part only asked about the moments right before the attempt, so essentially participants were only able to speak about that timeframe and not about the days, weeks, and months before. Second, for obvious reasons, the researchers were able to interview only individuals who survived their attempts. Given that the majority of non-fatal suicide attempts are intentional overdoses, but only around 16% of suicide deaths result from that method, it is reasonable to question whether asking survivors of attempts—a high percentage of which involved little chance of lethality—provides us much useful information about individuals who die by suicide. Indeed, our study also showed that how impulsive a person is in general did not differentiate those who died by suicide from living controls. Third, we noted that these studies did not consider episodic planning—thoughts that come and go rather than those that build up continuously until an event occurs.

To put this idea into context, imagine you go to your favorite restaurant for dinner one night. While there, you decide to treat yourself by placing a to-go order to save for lunch the next day. You rarely eat at this restaurant—the food is expensive and not healthy—so you are more excited than usual and at home that night spend a lot of time talking and thinking about tomorrow's lunch. The next morning, you pack up the meal and head to work. Shortly after arriving, you are inundated with unexpected calls and meetings, and work completely occupies your mind. In fact, the hours slip by in what feels like an instant and the entire time you do not think about your lunch even once. All of the sudden, you look at your clock and it is 3 p.m. You immediately heat up your meal and eat it, spending no more than a moment reflecting upon your decision to do so. Was reheating and eating your lunch at that moment an impulsive decision, or did it simply reflect a plan that was put in place but that evolved in response to all the other things going on in your life at that moment?

Some of my students and I published a smaller study more recently[24] in which we specifically asked about thoughts that came and went and found that among people who were certain that they wanted to die during their last suicide attempt, the most common response was that they first considered attempting suicide using their method of choice a year or more before the attempt. To be clear, it is not that they first thought about suicide at that point but rather they first started thinking about suicide using one specific method (e.g., a gun).

The other notable finding from this review—and the one most relevant to the ITS—was that in every study that has tested the possibility, researchers have found that the relationship between how impulsive people are and the extent to which they have engaged in suicidal behavior is explained by how many painful and life-threatening behaviors they have engaged in during their lives. In other words, impulsive people are more likely than non-impulsive people to encounter events that cause pain and threaten death or bodily harm—the very types of experiences that Joiner argues help an individual develop the capability for suicide. Impulsivity itself is not a path to suicidal behavior, it is one way that individuals overcome the fear of death over an extended period of time and, when that is paired with suicidal desire, danger increases substantially. All of this brings us back to a point I made earlier in the chapter—one that also contradicts the idea that suicide is cowardly and the easy way out: suicide is difficult. It is scary and often painful, and most of us simply cannot do it. When it happens, the evidence seems to indicate that it emerges slowly, after an individual in intense anguish has spent considerable time contemplating it and building up to it—either mentally or through actual practice (non-suicidal self-injury, for example). Most individuals simply are not capable of it, and for them the behavior never emerges. When it does, however, it tends to be a planned pursuit of death, not a frantic escape from life.

This debate has important implications for firearm suicides. I will explain more in chapter 3 how the capability is specifically relevant to the use of firearms, but it is worth taking a moment here to consider the clinical implications of suicide emerging impulsively. If people attempt suicide without planning ahead of time, detecting risk and preventing the behavior becomes much more difficult. If suicide is not impulsive, however, this means that the reason that we did not see it coming is not that it was unforeseeable, but rather because we either asked the wrong questions or the individual chose not to tell us about it. That second scenario does not sound particularly hopeful, but it offers more opportunities for us to save lives than the "impulsive" one does.

The take-home message of the ITS then is that people must desire and be capable of suicide in order to engage in a serious or lethal attempt. The notion that an individual must desire suicide to die is certainly not new, but the notion of a capability is—and its importance to our ability to understand and prevent suicide would be difficult to overstate. Joiner's words in *Why People Die by Suicide* articulated this notion when he noted, "When self-injury and other dangerous experiences become unthreatening and mundane—when people work up to the act of death by suicide by getting used to its threat and danger—that is when we might lose them" (p. 48). The theory fits the data well, helping us to understand why some individuals think about suicide but do not attempt whereas others attempt or even die by suicide. Our understanding of suicide through a framework such as the ITS provides us with an opportunity to better understand who is at the greatest risk of dying by suicide and how that risk developed. In the absence of such a theory, we are left to sort out a huge array of risk factors for suicide and data that in some ways can appear contradictory. With a theory such as this, we can understand risk factors as they apply to thinking about or engaging in suicidal behavior, and we can better understand our best opportunities for preventing that transition. I would forcefully argue that guns may represent the single biggest opportunity.

Three-Step Theory of Suicide

In 2014 David Klonsky of the University of British Columbia and one of his then doctoral students (now a PhD herself), Alexis May, published an article declaring the need for suicide research to consider everything through an "ideation to action" framework. By this they meant the very thing I have been talking about in this chapter: understanding how different characteristics and experiences influence the development of suicidal thoughts relative to the development of suicidal behavior. Klonsky and May noted that the ITS stands out as the first comprehensive theory to take this approach but also noted the need to continue challenging any framework and refining our understanding of suicide risk, just as Popper proposed as a central goal of any scientific theory.

In 2015 these same authors published an article describing their new theory of suicide, one they argue expands upon the ITS, while remaining consistent with its core message. Klonsky calls this theory the three-step theory of suicide, or 3ST, and its basic structure is not unlike that of the ITS. At its core, this theory argues that individuals start thinking about suicide when their pain—which could be physical, emotional, or both—is greater than their connectedness—which could involve connections to other people, a job, or other meaningful aspects of the individual's life. The theory further argues that people must be hopeless about the future for these sensations to prompt serious thoughts of suicide. This is not dissimilar to the ITS, but a primary difference is that although Klonsky agrees that thwarted belongingness and perceived burdensomeness are important and might be enough, he leaves the door open for other related but distinct experiences of pain to play that same role. Similar to the ITS, Klonsky also argues that a person must be capable of suicide for these thoughts of suicide to result in suicidal behavior. There is agreement between the two theories that the capability involves acquired and dispositional characteristics such as fearlessness about death and elevated pain tolerance, but Klonsky adds another element here that is particularly relevant to this book. He argues that the capability for suicide also involves practical factors related to an individual's access to and comfort with highly lethal means for suicide. In other words, no matter how fearless and pain tolerant you are, if you do not know how to use a gun or simply cannot access one (or another lethal method), you will not be capable of transitioning from ideation to action.

This might sound like a minor point—or even a commonsense one to some extent—but its implications are enormous and, in fact, lay the groundwork for much of what follows in this book. It matters if an individual has access to and familiarity with a specific method. If we can agree to that point, it then logically follows that our ability to manipulate that variable will have an enormous impact on the prevention of suicide. This means adjusting the way we think about suicide, acknowledging that much of what we think we "know" is actually wrong. In order to improve our suicide prevention efforts, we must start thinking much more about the specific ways in which people die.

Guns as a Powerful Force
in American Suicide

W HY DO I CLAIM THAT GUNS PLAY SUCH A MAJOR ROLE
in suicide rates when suicide is such a complicated issue? This
is an entirely reasonable question and one that should be asked by
folks on both sides of the debate to ensure that anti-gun sentiment is
not distorting our discussions on the subject any more than pro-gun
sentiments might. This chapter is devoted solely to answering this
question, starting with a review of data that paints a clear picture
of just how and why guns play such an enormous role in American
suicide rates. (Part of my answer will come in chapter 4, where I will
discuss why suicide is a gun issue and not simply a mental health
issue.)

Gun Ownership and Suicide

Over the past several decades scientists have studied the question of
whether access to guns increases risk for suicide. They have addressed
the question in a variety of ways, with the results of those studies
unambiguously supporting the idea that possessing a gun increases
the risk of death by suicide. However, I do not want you to simply take my word for it. Instead, I would like to walk you through

many of these findings so you can see how solid the evidence is for this claim.

In 2007 Robert Simon published a study demonstrating that suicide is five times more likely to occur in homes in which a gun is present, relative to homes in which there is no gun.[1] Alarming in its own right, this finding is actually less startling than one reported in 2001 by David Brent of Western Psychiatric Institute and Clinic in Pittsburgh. Brent found that the risk is even higher when the gun is stored unsafely, with the odds of suicide more than nine times greater when guns are stored loaded.[2] Findings such as those support the notion that having a gun around can, in some circumstances and for some individuals, prove dangerous, but they do not tell us how that danger develops. In an earlier study published in 1999, Garen Wintemute and colleagues demonstrated that the recent purchase of a gun is associated with an increased risk of suicide by any method—not just by firearms.[3] Findings such as this can seem confusing. After all, why would buying a gun have anything to do with a person's decision to hang himself, intentionally overdose, or jump from a high building? Although certainly not proven by that study, my suspicion is that the decision to buy the gun is sometimes a sign that a person is already suicidal and considering different ways in which he may be more comfortable attempting suicide. I do not suggest that all—or even most—individuals who buy a gun are doing so because they are acutely suicidal. I would, however, argue that acutely suicidal people are prone to thinking about and making efforts to acquire guns. They represent a small minority of those buying guns on any given day, but that minority is a critically meaningful one that we need to better understand.

In reality, many individuals who die by suicide using a gun had owned the gun for a long time prior to their deaths. So purchases are absolutely relevant, but they do not represent the entirety of the issue. This point is reflected in a range of scientific studies that have examined gun ownership more broadly as it relates to suicide. A rather large number of such studies have employed numerous approaches—looking at specific individuals or comparing suicide rates across the entire nation or within specific states or regions—to find repeatedly that gun ownership predicts death by suicide (or elevated overall suicide rates).[4-12] Much but not all of this research has been led by

Matthew Miller and his colleagues at Harvard University. Several other research groups have reported similar results.

If you are skeptical about the link between guns and suicide, you may wonder whether gun ownership itself is really the issue here or whether the findings are better explained by something else—and this is a reasonable reaction. Consider the classic example of the association between height and baldness. If you look only at large population numbers, you will see an undeniable association between height and baldness, such that the taller an individual is the greater the likelihood of baldness. But envision all the bald (and extraordinarily hairy) people you have encountered in life; it doesn't add up, does it? As it turns out, the taller you are, the more likely it is that you are male, and males are far more likely to be bald. So the association between height and baldness was actually just masking a more meaningful association—the one between baldness and whether one is male or female. Taller men are no more likely to be bald than are shorter men, and taller women are no more likely to be bald than are shorter women. It is simply a matter of height serving as a proxy for something else: sex.

Might a similar situation be at play here with guns and death by suicide? Fortunately, scientists have considered this possibility as well, and their results are once again clear. In fact, the researchers who conducted the studies I mentioned above have made an effort to control for the effects of other potentially important variables. What I mean is that, in running their analyses, scientists first factor in any association between other variables and death by suicide and then ask the data if gun ownership still predicts death by suicide. Using our earlier example, factoring in the effects of another variable (whether one is male or female) will completely eliminate the association between height and baldness. If that's not the case, however, then this is a sign that we either forgot to consider other important variables or that the relationship is important in its own right.

With gun ownership and suicide, researchers have controlled for mental illness (depression, substance use, etc.), the use of antidepressants, whether individuals are male or female, income levels, access to health care, state population, state population density, unemployment, prior thoughts of suicide, prior non-lethal suicide attempts, age, whether an individual lives alone or with others, education, and several other variables. To my knowledge, gun ownership has remained a significant predictor of death by suicide every single time, regardless of which of those variables is added to the equation. When we find an effect that many times after examining it from that many angles, it becomes increasingly difficult to make a solid case that it is not real. Even still, I frequently encounter individuals who question this association, so work on this issue remains active.

One of my doctoral students, Claire Houtsma, and I recently published a study examining the association between guns and suicide using more current data and considering an even wider range of possible alternative explanations than researchers did in the studies I already mentioned. Specifically, we looked at whether gun ownership predicted statewide overall suicide rates in 2013, even after controlling for statewide median age, the percentage of state residents over age 25 with a college education, the percentage of the population living under the poverty line, the percentage of the population identified as white, population density, the percentage of the population identifying as Christian, Jewish, Muslim, Buddhist, Hindu, Atheist, or Agnostic, the percentage of the population identifying as religiously unaffiliated, and the proportion of the state that identifies as military veterans. On top of that, we included statewide elevation, which some argue impacts how our brains process serotonin and dopamine and has demonstrated a remarkably strong association with statewide suicide rates.[13] Furthermore, we controlled for the effects of statewide rates of depression, drug or alcohol use disorders, serious mental illness, and serious suicidal ideation over the past year. Once we added in all of these variables, we accounted for more than 92% of the variability in statewide suicide rates. That means that nearly all the differences from state to state on suicide rates were accounted for by these variables, which is something we almost never see in social science research. Most importantly, even after we considered all of those other variables, gun ownership *still* predicted statewide suicide rates.[14] Looking at these numbers, it is simply not reasonable to dismiss the idea that guns play an important role in deaths by suicide that is not explained by other variables.

These findings do not represent the full picture of research on guns and suicide—I will be going into much more detail later—but they should explain why I claim that guns are one of the most important factors in American suicide. Taken together, what these studies have told us is that suicide is much more likely to occur in homes with guns, particularly if those guns are stored unsafely. This does not mean that suicide does not occur in homes without guns, but it tells us that the presence of a gun is relevant to the likelihood that somebody will die by suicide. These findings also tell us that the link between guns and suicide cannot simply be explained away by other factors, whether we are talking about mental illness, previous suicidal behavior, religious affiliation, geographic location, or demographics. All of those are pivotal considerations in their own right, but guns remain an important factor in death by suicide even after we work those variables into the equation.

Why are Guns So Important in Suicide?

While the findings discussed above rather unambiguously address the question of whether or not guns are relevant to suicide, they do not necessarily tell us much about why that association is there. The robust association of guns with suicide cannot be boiled down to one simple explanation, but I do believe there are several rather straight-forward considerations, each of which gives us at least part of the answer.

Guns are Highly Lethal

The first, and perhaps the most obvious, is the lethality of the method. It is difficult to calculate what percentage of suicide attempts result in death, as not all suicide attempts result in medical attention, and not all medically severe suicide attempts (or even deaths) are officially recorded as suicides. Many suicide attempts undoubtedly go unreported or are recorded as something else. Because of this, we must make educated guesses based on emergency room data (which only account for suicide attempts severe enough to warrant a visit to the ER), or by asking groups of people about their histories of suicide attempts; we then use those numbers to make estimates about the phenomenon as a whole. Both approaches come with their own set of strengths and weaknesses and neither produces perfectly accurate data, but they do provide rather clear evidence of one important point: far more often than not, people survive suicide attempts. I talked about this in chapter 2, when I noted that most individuals who think about suicide never make a suicide attempt, and most who make an attempt never die by suicide. This does not diminish the importance of suicidal thoughts, and it certainly does not indicate that suicide attempts are any less dangerous than most of us think they are. It simply demonstrates that suicide is difficult and that most efforts to die do not result in death.

One way to circumvent that trend is with a highly lethal method. Here is where guns stand out. Estimates from a range of studies indicate that suicide attempts involving a gun result in death somewhere between 85% and 95% of the time. In contrast, intentional overdoses—by far the most common suicide attempt method in the United States—are lethal only 2%–3% of the time. In other words, almost everyone who attempts suicide with a gun dies whereas almost everyone who attempts suicide by intentional overdose survives. So although guns are not used in suicide attempts all that often—less than 5% of all attempts by most estimates—they account for approximately half of all US suicide deaths because they are substantially more effective than most other methods.

As it turns out, highly lethal methods—whether they be guns, jumping from high places, or other frequently deadly approaches—are much less commonly used as suicide attempt methods than are generally non-lethal approaches. So should we then conclude that many people who attempt suicide do not really want to die and are merely making a "gesture" or seeking attention? Undoubtedly that happens on occasion, but there is clear evidence that whether or not people truly want to die during their suicide attempts is unrelated to the lethality of their chosen method (or how much medical attention they received). So this is not simply a matter of those who "truly" want to die picking the deadliest methods, nor of those who are ambivalent choosing methods less likely to prove lethal. Instead, all individuals who make suicide attempts are suffering immensely, with varying levels of true desire for death—and the level of suffering or certainty in their desire to die does not tell us much about the method they choose.

If you look at Table 3.1 you will notice that poisoning and cut/pierce injuries accounted for the greatest number of non-fatal self-injury episodes that resulted in emergency room attention in the year 2014. Poisoning can be thought of mainly as intentional overdoses,

TABLE 3.1 2014 Suicide Attempt Methods—How Lethal Were Specific Methods?

Method	Non-Fatal Self-Injury Events (% of injuries)	Death by Suicide Events (% of injuries)	% of Events Resulting in Death
Guns	3,320 (0.7%)	21,331 (49.9%)	86.5%
Suffocation	3,142 (0.7%)	11,407 (26.7%)	78.4%
Falling	3,311 (0.7%)	994 (2.3%)	23.1%
Cut/Pierce	112,845 (24.1%)	740 (1.7%)	0.7%
Poisoning	242,845 (51.6%)	6,808 (15.9%)	2.7%

Source: https://www.cdc.gov/injury/wisqars/index.html

whether those involve over the counter drugs or the misuse of prescription drugs, alone or in combination with another substance (e.g., alcohol). Cut/pierce wounds are most likely cutting wounds from non-suicidal self-injury rather than actual suicide attempts.[15] As I noted earlier, one of the big limitations of emergency room data in estimates of non-fatal suicide attempts is that they do not account for suicide attempts that did not result in an ER visit. We can assume that the vast majority of such attempts involved low lethality methods— likely self-poisoning with insufficient medication, or overdosing on medications unlikely to result in death—but we cannot know how many of them there were.

So what does this all mean? When people decide to kill themselves, by far the most likely approach will be an intentional overdose; however, this method is highly unlikely to kill them. In fact, if you look at the column on the far right of Table 3.1, you'll see again that less than 3% of all poisoning episodes that resulted in ER treatment were fatal, and remember that there were undoubtedly many other poisoning episodes that never resulted in admission to an ER. As such, a large proportion of those rare individuals able to transition from thinking about suicide to making a suicide attempt actually have a low likelihood of dying. Since up to 90% of individuals who make a suicide attempt never make another one, and among those who make multiple attempts the most common approach is to keep using the same method as in previous attempts, we have a situation in which most of the individuals in the "suicide attempt" group are unlikely to ever end up in the "firearm suicide attempt group."

The picture is quite different for firearms in Table 3.1. Less than 1% of non-fatal self-injury episodes resulting in ER treatment were due to self-inflicted gunshot wounds, but just shy of half of all suicide deaths resulted from this method. In this case, over 85% of all recorded instances of intentional self-inflicted gunshot wounds resulted in death. So bringing this back to the question of why guns are so important in suicide, we know that when individuals intentionally shoot themselves they almost always die. Also, and perhaps not surprisingly, the people most likely to shoot themselves are those who keep guns in their homes, particularly if those guns are stored unsafely. Here again it is worth noting that the vast majority of gun owners will never try to kill themselves, and simply owning a gun does not cause a person to become suicidal. But the data make a fairly clear statement that suicidal people in the presence of a gun are more likely to shoot themselves—and that when they do, they are likely to die.

Gun Ownership is Far More Common in the United States than Anywhere Else in the World

As I noted earlier, the question "Why are guns such an important factor in American suicide?" does not have one simple answer. Yes, the lethality of the method is an important component, and those data indicate that if more people used guns in suicide attempts, our national suicide rate would be even higher than it is right now. But this is only part of the story. Another explanation worth exploring is how prevalent guns are in America. The Small Arms Survey published work in August 2016 that examined civilian gun ownership worldwide.[16] In their write up, the authors noted that the United States accounts for less than 5% of the world's population but owns somewhere between 35% and 50% of all personal firearms worldwide. To add even more perspective, the authors estimated the number of firearms per 100 people in each country and reported that there are approximately 83 guns for every 100 people in the United States. Remarkably, the second highest level of per capita gun ownership was in Finland at 41, with Yemen at 32, Switzerland at 31, and

TABLE 3.2 Global Gun Ownership

Country	Population	Total Firearms	Firearms per 100 People
United States	300,000,000	270,000,000	83
Finland	5,210,000	2,900,000	41
Yemen	19,000,000	11,500,000	32
Switzerland	7,344,000	3,400,000	31
France	59,725,000	19,000,000	30

Source: Small Arms Survey (http://www.smallarmssurvey.org/fileadmin/docs/A-Yearbook/2007/en/full/Small-Arms-Survey-2007-Chapter-02-EN.pdf)

France at 30 guns per 100 persons rounding out the top five. This means that the United States has twice as many guns per capita than the second highest-ranked country and nearly three times as many as the country ranked third. Also consider that whereas the United States has approximately 300 million citizens, the other countries in the top five have far fewer. As a result, these numbers translate to the United States having an estimated 270 million privately owned guns within its borders, as compared to 2.9 million in Finland, 11.5 million in Yemen, 3.4 million in Switzerland, and 19 million in France (see Table 3.2). In other words, the United States has seven times as many guns as the next top-four countries on that list combined.

Given these numbers, it becomes rather clear that the United States has more exposure and access to guns than do people anywhere else in the world. When we look more closely at the state level, the picture gets even more interesting, as gun ownership rates vary widely from state to state (and, in some cases, county to county or town to city). In a recent study led by Bindu Kalesan of Columbia University,[17] this point was demonstrated quite clearly (see Table 3.3).

As you can see from Table 3.3, the percentage of gun-owning citizens in a given state varies widely, with Alaska coming in with the highest rate at 61.7% and Delaware coming in at the lowest with 5.2%. What the Kalesan study does not tell us is how many guns each individual gun owner possesses, which makes it impossible to accurately guess the total number of guns in the nation. I took a conservative approach here though and calculated the total number of guns in each state if each gun owner possesses only one gun. To me,

TABLE 3.3 Total Gun Estimates in High and Low Gun Ownership States

State	Population	% Owning a Gun	# of Guns if One Gun Per Owner
Five States with the Highest Gun Ownership Rate			
Alaska	736,732	61.7%	454,564
Arkansas	2,966,369	57.9%	1,717,527
Idaho	1,634,464	56.9%	930,010
West Virginia	1,850,326	54.2%	1,002,876
Wyoming	584,153	53.8%	314,274
Five States with the Lowest Gun Ownership Rate			
Delaware	935,614	5.2%	48,652
Rhode Island	1,055,173	5.8%	61,200
New York	19,746,227	10.3%	2,033,861
New Jersey	8,938,175	11.3%	1,010,013
New Hampshire	1,326,813	14.4%	191,061

Source: Kalesan, B., Villarreal, M.D., Keyes, K.M., & Galea, S. (in press). Gun ownership and social gun culture. Injury Prevention. Available early online at: http://injuryprevention.bmj.com/content/early/2015/06/09/injuryprev-2015-041586.abstract

the most interesting piece of information that emerges from Table 3.3 is that New York, despite having the third lowest gun ownership rate in the country, is estimated to have nearly as many guns as Finland, which is the country with the second highest rate of guns per capita in the world (and again, this is probably an enormous understatement, as it assumes each New York gun owner only has one gun). Because our population and gun ownership rates are so high, even states with low gun ownership rates relative to other states still have a lot of guns. Put simply, guns are omnipresent in our country, in our own homes, and in the images and stories that permeate our literature and popular media.

The right to own a gun is a fiercely debated issue in America. That debate causes such an emotional response in so many that political candidates routinely mention threats to it in an effort to steer the media narrative and energize their base. With respect to suicide, I would argue that this places the United States in a unique position of risk. I spent a good deal of time in chapter 2 discussing the notion of the capability for suicide. In both Joiner's and Klonsky's models of suicide risk, the argument is that individuals who desire suicide must also be capable of suicide in order to make that rare transition from thinking about suicide to engaging in a suicide attempt (and particularly the transition to making a fatal suicide attempt). Klonsky made two particularly important additions to the idea of the capability for suicide when he introduced his Three Step Theory of suicide in 2015. One, as I mentioned in the previous chapter, is the notion that an individual must develop comfort and aptitude with a specific lethal method for suicide in order to engage in a lethal attempt. No matter how badly people want to die, if they do not have experience and comfort with their chosen method, the odds of them engaging in the attempt are much lower, which at least partially explains why the most common suicide attempt method involves ingesting medication (which nearly all of us have done several times by the time we are adolescents). In a nation inundated with guns, the opportunity to become comfortable and familiar with firing a gun is drastically increased. The simple logistic barrier of not possessing or knowing how to properly use a gun is much less imposing in the United States than it is in other countries, and as a result it becomes easier for suicidal Americans to develop a suicide plan involving a gun and to implement that plan. Corroborating this notion, in a project that my colleague Dan Capron and I recently published, we found that the number of times people have fired a gun is significantly associated with their pain tolerance, fearlessness about death, and lifetime number of suicide attempts. Importantly, our sample was collected in Mississippi, a particularly high gun ownership state, thereby highlighting that this issue is relevant not only in places in which guns are uncommon.[18]

A second innovation put forth by Klonsky, albeit one that has not yet been rigorously tested, is the notion that hearing about the suicide death of another individual temporarily increases one's capability for suicide by infusing him with the sense that he might be able to die by suicide, too. Given that half or more of all suicides in the United States result from gunshot wounds, this means that gun-specific temporary increases in the capability for suicide are more common in the United States than anywhere else in the world. As such, an American—suffering, isolated, and hopeless about his future—may develop thoughts of suicide, with a certainty that his own death would bring relief to others. That individual, living in a country with far more guns than any other in the world, surrounded by images and stories of gun violence and likely with knowledge of some other person—a peer or maybe a celebrity—who died by suicide using a gun, may find it easier to consider and ultimately approach and implement a plan to die from a self-inflicted gunshot wound. This is not to say that guns create a suicide "contagion" effect but rather that suicidal people in the United States are exposed to firearms—and firearm suicides—far more often than are people in other countries, and such exposure may fuel temporary but meaningful increases in the capability for suicide that facilitate the transition from suicidal thought to suicidal behavior.

Now, an argument could be made that a gun itself does not facilitate suicidal behavior and that, instead, cultural norms or an individual's beliefs are more important. I am not unmoved by that notion and, in fact, I think that this possibility could be leveraged in suicide prevention efforts I propose in chapter 7. That being said, the undeniable truth is that without access to a gun—or at least without quick and easy access to an unsafely stored gun—logistical barriers would be in place that would lower the odds of a suicidal individual carrying out a plan to die by suicide. As such, in addition to the simple lethality of the method, the omnipresence of guns helps explain why they are so important in American suicide.

Isn't This Just a Mental Health Problem, not a Gun Problem?

S PEAKING TO CNN ABOUT GUN VIOLENCE IN AUGUST 2015, then-Republican presidential candidate Donald Trump said, "This isn't a gun problem, this is a mental problem."[1] This refrain has become a common one, so much so that a quick Google search for political opinions on gun violence will reveal countless references to the quote "It's a mental health problem" without any attribution to a source. It's not clear exactly where this belief came from, but it permeates the political discourse. The idea that gun violence is a "mental health problem" rests on the notion that it is unreasonable to blame the gun itself for the outcome—whether referencing homicide or suicide—or to assume its absence would have prevented it (remember "Guns don't kill people, people kill people"?). Instead, gun violence is seen as an inevitable result of mental illness and a failure on the part of the mental health-care system to adequately treat those likely to harm themselves or others with a gun. On the eve of the 2016 State of the Union address, and in response to President Obama's executive orders on background checks, NRA director of public affairs Jennifer Baker said, "If you look at the data and the sheer number of increases in suicides, including suicides carried out by means other than firearms, it is very clear that a solution that would actually save lives is dealing with the mental health issue. Gun control is not the answer."[2]

At face value, the contention that gun violence is a mental health issue seems fairly reasonable, at least for suicide. The general reasoning is that mental illness is the underlying cause of suicidal behavior and that the gun is simply one of many instruments an individual could have chosen to cause his or her own death. The gun itself is not the problem, goes this line of thinking, so a focus on guns represents a prevention effort too far along in the process of emerging suicide risk, with a low probability of sustained value. Although I will discuss in much greater detail later how theory and data have dispelled this prospect, it bears emphasizing here: those who promote the idea that gun violence is not a gun problem frequently (and incorrectly) assert that a focus on the gun is problematic because an individual who is suicidal and thwarted in his or her effort to use a gun in a suicide attempt will simply find another way to die.

Further boosting the notion that gun violence is a mental health issue, many experts have cited a finding that 90% of those who die by suicide have a diagnosable mental illness,[3] and some argue that the number should actually be 100%.[4] If we accept those numbers—and there is no compelling reason that we should not—then it is entirely reasonable to assume that mental illness is a factor in suicide. Few if any suicide researchers would dispute this point.

As I discussed at length earlier, however, it is important to remember that a variable being "associated with suicide," is a rather vague notion that provides us with minimal useful information. Mental illnesses are associated with suicide without question, but *how* they are associated with *specific aspects* of suicide risk is the more meaningful—and complicated—issue. Let's take depression as an example. Using data from the National Comorbity Survey Replication (NCS-R), Ronald Kessler of Harvard University and several of his colleagues found that 6.6% of adults in the United States typically experience a major depressive episode in any given year, with 16.2% reporting an episode at some point in their lives.[5] Those numbers may appear insignificant, but for comparison's sake, the American Diabetes Association reported that 9.3% of the U.S. population was living with diabetes,[6] and the CDC reported that 3.8% of

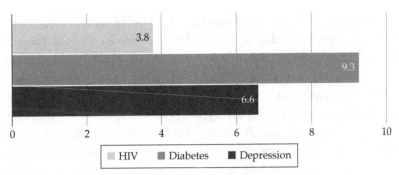

FIGURE 4.1 Percent of Americans Experiencing Specific Illnesses
Each Year.

Sources: (1) Kessler, R.C., Berglund, P., Demler, O., Jin, R., Koretz, D.,
Merikangas, K.R., et al. (2003). The epidemiology of major depressive
disorder: Results from the National Comorbidity Survey Replication (NCS-R).
JAMA, 289, 3095–3105.
(2) http://www.diabetes.org/diabetes-basics/statistics/
(3) http://www.cdc.gov/hiv/statistics/overview/

the population qualified as HIV positive[7] in 2012 (see Figure 4.1). The
percentages are small, but they are higher than other common public
health problems in the United States, and the raw numbers are enormous, which means many Americans are currently or will at some
point be suffering through a bought of depression.

Most relevant to the point, depression has also repeatedly been
shown to be elevated in individuals who die by suicide relative to
individuals who do not. In fact, data going back more than half a
century have revealed that depression is the most common mental illness diagnosed in those who die by suicide.[8] When we look
a bit more closely at the data, however, things are not that simple.
Again using data from the National Comorbidity Survey (NCS) and
NCS-R, researchers led by Guilherme Borges found that although
depression predicted the experience of suicidal ideation (suicidal
thoughts) during the 10 years between the NCS and NCS-R, it
was unrelated to the occurrence of suicidal *behavior* (actual suicide
attempts).[9] So depression prompts thoughts of suicide but does not
necessarily prompt the transition from ideation to attempt. Taking
this point even further, Borges and colleagues found that no single mental illness or combination of mental illnesses predicted suicide attempts during the 10 years between the initial NCS and the
follow-up NCS-R.

Thinking back to the theories of Thomas Joiner and David Klonsky, remember that serious or lethal suicidal behavior requires not only the desire for suicide but also the capability to act on suicidal thoughts. Although thought of by many as an "easy way out," suicide is actually extraordinarily difficult. Most who think about suicide do not have the capability to act on those thoughts, and most who are capable of suicide do not have suicidal thoughts. It is the relatively rare convergence of desire and capacity that results in the greatest risk of somebody attempting and then dying by suicide. Mental illness alone—at least according to the data—does not seem to confer the capability for suicide. Feeling depressed can stem from or cause social isolation and a belief that others would be better off if you were gone; and such sensations—when they seem intractable—can prompt thoughts of suicide.[10] That being said, nothing in that sequence speaks to the variables that Joiner, Klonsky, and others have shown to be vital components of the capability for suicide: elevated pain tolerance, fearlessness about death, and access to and familiarity with lethal means. Put another way, depression might make an individual want to die by suicide, but it does not make this difficult goal easier to achieve.

So why is depression more common in individuals who die by suicide? Because suicide attempts will not occur without suicidal thoughts, and depression promotes those thoughts. Most people experiencing those thoughts do not attempt suicide, and most who attempt suicide do not die. But because those who think about suicide, on average, have higher levels of depression than individuals who do not think about suicide (and because all individuals who die by suicide had thoughts of suicide), simple arithmetic tells us that depression rates will be higher in those who died by suicide than in those who did not. This does not, however, mean that the depression explains the outcome. If it did, a much higher percentage of depressed individuals (or even more conservatively, depressed individuals with thoughts of suicide) would attempt and ultimately die by suicide.

Why Not Focus on Mental Health Care Rather than Targeting One Specific Method for Suicide?

When politicians and gun rights advocates state that gun violence as it relates to suicide is "a mental health issue," I suspect they are referring less to the data above linking specific diagnoses to thoughts versus behavior and more to the utility of focusing on mental health care rather than guns themselves in suicide prevention efforts. Here again, at face value, it seems a reasonable point is being made. After all, increasing the quality of care for individuals in need is an obvious way to help those individuals recover more fully and avoid adverse health outcomes. My contention, however, is that although efforts to improve the mental health-care system are sorely needed and would help many people currently suffering with suboptimal or absent care, this approach would largely fail to help the populations most at risk for suicide (particularly suicide by gun) and, as such, would ultimately fall short of the goal of drastically reducing the national suicide rate.

The suicide prevention community has, in many ways, embraced the importance of expanding and improving upon mental health-care services through the development of a range of evidence-based treatment and prevention approaches specifically designed for individuals with elevated suicide risk. The most prominent example is Marsha Linehan's Dialectical Behavior Therapy (DBT).[11] DBT was initially designed to treat suicidal women diagnosed with borderline personality disorder; however, its utility has been tested in much more diverse groups of suicidal individuals over the past two decades. DBT involves both individual and group therapy sessions focused on developing skills for managing chronic and acute distress, problematic interpersonal interactions, and impulsive decision making. Numerous high-quality randomized controlled trials (RCTs) have shown that the treatment is effective in reducing non-suicidal self-injury, inpatient hospitalization, and suicide attempts.[12] Recent work has demonstrated that the group skills training component on its own may be as effective as the full treatment[13], introducing the possibility that the treatment could be reduced in length and potentially delivered over shorter periods, perhaps even through smart phone apps rather than in-person interactions. In this sense, an already powerful treatment may have the potential to reach a broader audience that either does not have access to full DBT or is disinclined to seek outpatient treatment.

Similarly promising results have been found recently for brief cognitive behavioral therapy (BCBT)[14] for suicidal soldiers, a protocol developed by psychologists David Rudd and Craig Bryan, among others. In a recent RCT, these authors demonstrated a 60% reduction in suicidal behavior among soldiers who received BCBT and treatment as usual relative to those receiving only treatment as usual.[15] Suicidal soldiers, at least demographically, represent a group of individuals that differs substantially from the women for whom DBT was originally designed to treat: this is a point that highlights the versatility of current evidence-based treatments for suicidality.

Evidence-based treatments such as DBT and BCBT represent vital advances in the prevention of suicide and the results from well-designed RCTs speak to the value of providing these services to suicidal individuals. Their success also seems to support the idea that our best path forward in suicide prevention is through focusing on mental health. As wonderful as these tools are, however, their development and gradual implementation has coincided with a continued rise in the national suicide rate. According to CDC data, the U.S. suicide rate increased by 28.2% from 1999 (10.46 per 100,000) to 2014 (13.41 per 100,000), with increases in each year since 2005. In contrast, other public health problems have seen substantial reductions in rates over similar timeframes. For instance, the rate of new cases of lung cancer dropped by 17.2% from 1999 (65.8 per 100,000) to 2012 (54.5 per 100,000)[16]. Similarly, the rate of motor vehicle deaths dropped by 29.9% from 2005 (14.7 per 100,000) to 2013 (10.3 per 100,000)[17] (see Figure 4.2).

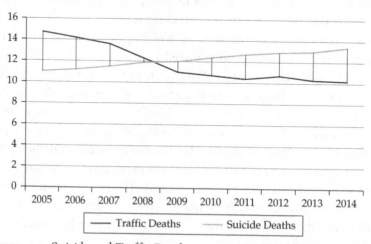

FIGURE 4.2 Suicide and Traffic Deaths per 100,000 American, 2005–2014.

Sources: (1) http://www.iihs.org/iihs/topics/t/general-statistics/fatalityfacts/state-by-state-overview/2013
(2) https://www.cdc.gov/injury/wisqars/index.html

The continual rise in the suicide rate thus represents an unfortunate contrast to the progress we have made in other areas of public health in recent years. Given the impressive findings for evidence-based treatments for suicidality, these numbers are rather startling, and they point to a troubling deficiency in our suicide prevention efforts. If these tools represent the bulk of what we need to prevent suicide, the primary outcome they aim to address—the occurrence of suicide—would not be increasing every year. We need more tools—and better ones.

Why Evidence-based Mental Health Treatments Have Failed to Lower the Suicide Rate

I contend that guns explain a sizable portion of the discrepancy between our continuously improving suicide prevention programs and our rising national suicide rate. To understand my rationale, it is important to first consider who the individuals are that are most likely to die by suicide using a gun. Among the 21,334 firearm suicides in the United States in 2014, 92.7% of the decedents were white, and 85.9% were male. Additionally, despite accounting for only 14.5% of the total U.S. population, older adults (aged 65+) accounted for 25.2% of the firearm suicides. Among older adult suicide deaths, 91.5% of the decedents were male.[18] These numbers point to an elevated propensity on the part of men in general to use guns in suicide attempts, with this being particularly true for older adult males. A similar trend can be seen in military personnel, including reservists, National Guard personnel, active duty soldiers, and veterans.

The pronounced sex differences in suicide deaths—both overall (77.4% male) and specifically with respect to firearms (85.9% male)—stand in stark contrast to nonfatal suicide attempt numbers. By most estimates, women account for 75%–80% of all nonlethal suicide attempts, meaning women are far more likely to desire and attempt suicide, but men are far more likely to die from it (see Table 4.1).

Much as was the case in our discussion of the role of depression in suicide, the reason for this disparity likely centers on the capability for suicide. The three most commonly cited components of the capability for suicide—increased pain tolerance, increased fearlessness about death, and access to and familiarity with lethal means—show distinct patterns in men relative to women. Men, on average, exhibit

TABLE 4.1 Sex Differences in Suicidal Behavior

Non-lethal Suicide Attempts	75–80% Female
Deaths by Suicide	77% Male
Firearm Suicides	86% Male

Women are far more likely to think about and attempt suicide
Men are far more likely to die by suicide

Source: https://www.cdc.gov/injury/wisqars/index.html

higher levels of pain tolerance[19] and fearlessness about death[20] than do women. For older adults, this can be explained in part through a lifetime of exposure to the types of painful and/or provocative experiences capable of impacting pain tolerance and an increased acceptance of mortality. In soldiers, this has been explored in the work of Craig Bryan and his colleagues, who found that U.S. Air Force personnel who had recently completed basic training were less fearful of death than civilians—even civilians with multiple prior suicide attempts (a large majority of the soldiers were male and a large majority of the civilians were female).[21] My doctoral student Brittney Assavedo recently replicated this finding in a sample of Army National Guard personnel as well.[22] Recent research has also shown that adherence to masculine gender norms, such as restrictive emotionality and an emphasis on success, money, and power, is associated with the capability for suicide in large part because individuals who adopt such norms tend to engage in more painful and/or provocative experiences.[23] Men are also far more likely than women to own personal firearms,[24] and here again the pattern is amplified further in the military, where individuals receive extensive training in the use of guns. Taken together, the emerging pattern is one of men being far more likely than women to die by suicide—particularly with respect to firearms—and this difference likely being at least partially a function of the fact that men are typically less likely to think about suicide but more capable of transitioning from suicidal thoughts to fatal suicidal behavior.

There is another set of variables on which women differ from men in general and from the specific groups of men discussed above: the utilization of mental health-care resources and the willingness to report thoughts of suicide. Women are far more likely than men to seek mental health services.[25] Given that 85.9% of firearm suicide deaths in 2014 were men, this obviously represents a problem. Similarly, older adults have been shown to underreport suicidal ideation relative to younger adults,[26] so even if an older adult male does seek out mental health services—which happens, but at a much lower rate than in many other demographic groups—he is still unlikely to report thoughts of suicide.

Kelly Cukrowicz of Texas Tech University and several of her colleagues demonstrated this point remarkably well using an advanced statistical technique referred to as zero-inflated negative binomial regression.[27] This approach allows scientists to look at variables in which a large portion of a group score zero, a common occurrence on measures of suicidal ideation because most people at any given moment are not thinking about suicide. With this technique, researchers can use scores on other related measures—factors such as social isolation, feelings of burdensomeness, and hopelessness—to predict the likelihood that particular individuals would score zero on the other measure (suicidal thoughts). The model essentially demonstrates that given elevated scores on specific variables or combinations of variables, it would run counter to expectations for an individual not to be experiencing any thoughts of suicide. Cukrowicz found that given their scores on scales that measure things such as social isolation, many of the older adults who reported no suicidal thoughts were unlikely to be truly free of suicidal ideation. In other words, a sizable number of older adults in this study reported difficulties in interpersonal relationships and a sense of being a drain on others but seemed to falsely deny the suicidal thoughts likely to accompany such feelings in many individuals. Although this certainly is not a tool with which to conclusively identify specific individuals who are being dishonest about their thoughts, it does compellingly support the notion that older adults are open about some topics (feeling isolated) but less so about others (suicidal thoughts). The implications of this finding for suicide risk assessments in older adults are enormous, as denial of current suicidal ideation typically results in an individual being judged as low risk for suicide.

The same point holds true for military personnel. The military promotes a "warrior culture"[28] in which soldiers are trained to push through distress, solve their personal problems on their own, and take all necessary steps to avoid being separated from their units. In many aspects of a military career, this approach is remarkably beneficial—perhaps even lifesaving. Within the context of suicide risk, however, a case could be made that such a culture is more problematic. Indeed, past studies have shown that soldiers tend to view mental health difficulties as a sign of weakness[29] and are suspicious of mental health-care providers, particularly those outside the military.[30] Compounding this issue is the logistical barrier of reduced confidentiality. When soldiers report thoughts of suicide, such reports become part of their permanent record and can influence, among other things, promotion opportunities and the extent to which fellow members of the soldier's unit interact with and trust the soldier in certain situations. Soldiers have thus reported a fear that endorsing any difficulties with mental health would have an adverse impact on their careers. Unsurprisingly, soldiers have also been found to underreport suicidal ideation. As one example, my colleague Brad Green and I collected data from approximately 1,000 soldiers, nearly all of whom were affiliated with the Army National Guard. The clinical utility of examining a sample such as ours is highlighted by the fact that the Army National Guard has the highest suicide rate of all U.S. military branches and components (33.4 per 100,000 in 2013[31]) and is further underscored by the fact that nearly half of those soldiers were demobilizing from deployment to a war zone at the time of the assessment.

In our survey, we included two separate measures, or questionnaires, of current thoughts of suicide. We informed the soldiers that the first measure was a part of our safety protocol and that their answers would be used to determine imminent risk to self. The soldiers knew that they ran the risk of being reported to onsite military mental health personnel if their responses on that measure were deemed indicative of imminent risk of self-harm. The second measure, however, was not a part of the safety protocol and, as such, soldiers were made aware that their answers would not be reported to the military. The difference in confidentiality substantially impacted willingness to report, with an increase of 57% in endorsements of ideation in the more confidential measure (n = 67) relative to the less confidential measure (n = 45).[32] Taking this a step further, several colleagues and I are currently working on an analysis that parallels that of Cukrowicz and colleagues: our results indicate that even on the more confidential measure a substantial portion of the soldiers may have been underreporting thoughts of suicide.

Although I certainly would not argue against improvements in our mental health-care system as a way to improve other mental health outcomes, the data described above indicate that the individuals most likely to die by suicide using a gun may be disinclined to report suicidal thoughts at all—even in such an improved system, and assuming they choose to even engage with the system at all. In the absence of willingness to seek out help and openly report suicidal thoughts, individuals at high risk for suicide are unlikely to come to the attention of health-care providers prior to their deaths. As it stands, our most effective treatments for suicide risk focus on the treatment of suicidal desire. This has repeatedly proven useful for many suffering openly with suicidal thoughts, but such approaches also depend upon people to seek and openly engage with help, and all of the evidence I have discussed so far indicates that this simply is not a realistic expectation for many of those most vulnerable to firearm suicides (and indeed, suicide by any method).

Can Intervention after Non-lethal Suicide Attempts Decrease Firearm Suicides?

Another approach to the identification of individuals at high risk for suicide is through contact with the mental health-care system as a result of a nonlethal suicide attempt. In theory, those who under-report suicidal ideation may ultimately make a suicide attempt, and given that there are, on average, at least 13 nonlethal suicide attempts for every death by suicide,[33] most of those individuals will survive and become more readily identifiable as high risk. As an example, a person who has never been in therapy, or has never been given a mental health diagnosis (but who survives an intentional overdose of medication), could end up in an emergency room as a result of the attempt. Depending upon the severity of the attempt, the state and hospital the individual was treated in, and a variety of other factors, the person might end up spending several days in an inpatient psychiatric unit. Once he or she is deemed to no longer be at imminent risk to self, that person will be released back into the community. At this point, even if referrals to mental health care have not been made, members of the individual's support system (friends, family, etc.) are likely now aware of the situation and more apt to be vigilant for signs of risk (and to offer social support, an important protective factor for suicidal ideation). In this sense, the nonfatal attempt becomes the entry point for a previously unidentified high-risk individual and an opportunity to engage with him despite his previous efforts to avoid the mental health-care system. This approach has potential value in that prior suicide attempts are one of the most robust predictors of future death by suicide,[34] and a lifetime history of suicide attempts (particularly *multiple* past attempts) is one of the most important factors in assessing a person's suicide risk.[35]

Although this scenario has some relevance to our discussion of guns and suicide, it would still fall far short as a leading technique with which to identify those at risk and to intervene. As much as those most vulnerable to death by suicide using a gun often avoid mental health services and deny suicidal ideation, it occurred to me that such people may avoid detection for another reason altogether: the effectiveness of guns as a method for suicide. To test this notion, I consulted data from the National Violent Death Reporting System (NVDRS). The NVDRS is a voluntary reporting system into which participating states enter data regarding violent deaths of residents, with details that range from circumstance (e.g., homicide, suicide) to method (e.g., firearm, intentional overdose) to contextual factors (e.g., did the individual leave a note, or have any prior suicide attempts?). Currently, only 17 states take part in the NVDRS, and within each of those states not all deaths are reported, and not all reported deaths have sufficient data available to address all of the questions. Nonetheless, the system offers a wealth of data that is otherwise hard to obtain. And with a recent push to expand participation, the NVDRS may soon become an even more valuable resource. In this project, I consulted data from 2005 through 2012 and looked at whether suicide decedents who died using a gun were any less likely than suicide decedents who died by other methods to have made a prior suicide attempt (by any method—not simply by guns, which are almost always fatal). The idea here was that if firearm suicide decedents tend to die by suicide on their first attempt more often than do suicide decedents who die using other methods, then members of this particular group would be less likely to come to our attention prior to death and would thus be more difficult to identify. I was able to look at more than 70,000 individuals who died by suicide—more than half of whom died from a gunshot wound—and the results were consistent with my expectations. Whereas 28.7% of suicide decedents who died by a method other than a gun had a prior suicide attempt before their fatal attempt, only 12.1% of firearm suicide decedents had a prior attempt.[36]

This finding indicates that in addition to their tendency to underutilize mental health-care resources and underreport suicidal ideation, firearm suicide decedents are highly unlikely to end up in contact with mental health resources following the survival of a nonlethal attempt. Nearly 90% of the firearm decedents in the NVDRS sample died during their *first* suicide attempt. This means that a system built on preventing death through an understanding of current suicidal ideation and prior suicidal behavior is rather ill-equipped to identify and help those most at risk for dying by suicide using a gun—by far the most common form of suicide death in the United States.

Increased Reach and Quality of Mental Health Care Will Not Solve the Problem of Suicide

The notion that firearm suicides are a "mental health problem" and not a "gun problem"—intuitively appealing as it may be to many— starts to fall apart when you pull all of these findings together. The individuals most likely to die by suicide using a gun—and remember that this group represents both the majority of gun deaths and the majority of suicides—are highly unlikely to flock to even an improved and expanded mental health-care system. So the underreporting of suicidal thoughts is not an issue of access to or quality of care. It is an issue of a potential suicide victim not wanting to tell anyone that they are seriously thinking about suicide.

To be clear, again I am not promoting the idea that expanding and improving our mental health-care system would not be worthwhile. In fact, I believe that if our government adopted a system similar to that of the United Kingdom, where evidence-based mental health care is the standard and is substantially more accessible, we would see a profound impact on the prognosis for individuals with mental illnesses. That does not necessarily speak to the prevention of the initial onset of those conditions, but it certainly means that a massive number of individuals could reclaim their lives and recover from suffering. Along these lines, I also want to be clear that I am not arguing that improvements upon and expansion of the mental health-care system would be irrelevant to suicide prevention. Here again, I think that such a shift could make a meaningful difference in suicide-related outcomes. The problem is that according to the data reviewed earlier, such improvement would largely benefit individuals vulnerable to dying by suicide using means other than a gun. Remember that women are far more likely to utilize mental health-care resources than men are. They are also substantially more likely to think about and attempt suicide. But by far the most common attempt method for women is intentional overdose, and as I noted in chapter 3, approximately 98% of intentional overdoses are nonfatal. An improvement in our mental health-care system would be greatly beneficial to those seeking such services and those vulnerable to utilizing less lethal means in suicide attempts (who are thus more likely to arrive in emergency rooms for acute care after a suicide attempt). This would represent an invaluable step forward for our country, but it would likely fail to help many Americans who use a gun to end their own lives.

There is also good reason to be skeptical about what politicians and policymakers mean when they talk about expanding and improving our mental health-care system. For one thing, mental health providers rarely use evidence-based treatments. Indeed, research has shown that, despite the existence of effective front line psychotherapies for the treatment of both posttraumatic stress disorder (prolonged exposure and cognitive processing therapy) and obsessive compulsive disorder (exposure and ritual prevention), the large majority of therapists who treat such patients do not use these approaches.[37,38] As the brilliant Scott Lilienfeld has noted,[39] this phenomenon extends across a range of diagnoses, with most patients with autism spectrum disorders receiving ineffective and/or untested treatments such as facilitated communication[40], individuals with eating disorders receiving a range of pseudoscientific treatments such as equine-assisted psychotherapy[41] and countless other examples.

The lack of mental health practitioners providing proper mental health care is compounded by the fact that the very idea of evidence-based treatments for mental illness is unfamiliar to many mental health-care consumers. In other words, the lack of supply is compounded by a lack of demand. If providers are offering low-quality treatment options and consumers are not demanding anything different, expansion of the mental health-care system without a massive revision to the process driven by scientifically minded approaches seems vulnerable to introducing an influx of services incapable of addressing mental health problems. When politicians speak about mental health and mental health care, this point rarely if ever comes up. We as a country have come to expect that other aspects of safety and health care—whether this means the safety measures installed in our automobiles or the procedures involved in specific surgical approaches—are based upon a careful study of the topic by experts and clear evidence that these are, in fact, the best available options. But this is not the case with mental health care. As a result, in addition to the general reluctance among those most likely to die by suicide using a gun to even engage with the mental health-care system, there is the added concern that if they do actually engage, the help they receive will be insufficient.

Suicide, firearms, mental illness, and mental health care are all highly fraught topics, and the arguments I have made here may meet with resistance or even dismay and anger. In response, I suggest that some distress might be necessary in order to help shift the focus of suicide prevention from the realm of politics and gut feelings to the realm of careful science and investigation of what actually works. I wholeheartedly believe in the expansion of mental health care, but that expansion must be entirely focused on an established evidence base demonstrating that specific approaches work for specific problems. I also believe that any such expansion needs to occur with an understanding that it will largely fail to account for the tens of thousands of Americans who kill themselves with a gun each year. These people need help, but it must come in a different form than what we are currently offering. In the following chapters I will describe several options available and the convincing evidence that they represent our best hope of saving more people from firearm suicides.

Part II
The Solution

Lowering the National Suicide Rate Requires Means Safety

IN THE FIRST HALF OF THIS BOOK, MY GOAL WAS TO explain why I believe guns are such an important factor in American suicide. In doing so, my hope was not to villainize guns or gun owners or to oversimplify the tragedy of suicide but rather to make the case that guns represent an opportunity we as a nation can leverage in a concerted effort to substantially lower the national suicide rate. On its own, the first half of the book serves a worthwhile purpose—highlighting important facts about suicide that I believe have largely been overlooked—but to some extent also represents an empty complaint. I clearly remember a moment during my first semester of graduate school when Thomas Joiner talked to us about the most effective ways to make an impact as a scientist. He told us it is easy to be a critic, but he also noted that criticism has little to no value in the absence of proposed solutions. If I were merely to point out a problem without making any tangible suggestions as to what to do about it, this book would be ineffectual. We would be left with the knowledge that the building is on fire without knowing how to get out, nor whether there was hope of salvaging the structure.

The second half of the book will thus forge a path forward. Equipped with the knowledge that suicide is a public health crisis and that guns play an enormous role in the problem, I argue that there are tangible steps we can take that could legitimately decrease the rate at which Americans die by suicide each year. To be clear, I am not proposing that these solutions—focused entirely on guns—will eliminate suicide or that they should replace traditional psychotherapy and psychopharmacology. Rather, the measures that follow are intended as a vital component of a larger suicide prevention system. These suggestions stand out, however, because they differ so greatly from the approaches we currently use. They also have the potential to reach people who otherwise will not engage with the mental health-care system. The most effective psychotherapy is useless if men and women struggling with suicidal thoughts never come to the therapy room. For a variety of reasons, whether it has to do with stigma, finances, physical access to care, religious views about mental illness and the best path to wellness (or any other factors), the fact is that many of those suffering with suicidal thoughts will never seek help or tell others about their thoughts and plans. The ideas that follow are not irrelevant to those who do seek help for their suicidal thoughts, but their primary value lies in their potential to dramatically lower the suicide risk levels of those people we do not even know are struggling, as well as those who simply decide against seeking help.

In the summer of 2016, my doctoral students and I published a paper in the journal *Suicide and Life-Threatening Behavior* that I think sets the stage for my proposed solutions quite well.[1] In this paper we argued that although there are wonderfully effective therapies for suicidal individuals, such therapies are plainly not adequately addressing the problem because the national suicide rate is still increasing. If they were doing with 100% effectiveness what they were intended to do, the development and dissemination of such treatments would correspond to a reduction in suicides. This scenario came about in part, we argued, because the tools we currently use on a large scale—all of which focus entirely on decreasing an individual's *suicidal desire* with no consideration of their *capability* for suicide—rely upon those suffering to seek help. Furthermore, within a treatment landscape dominated by ineffective and untested therapies, our nation's current approach to suicide reduction further depends upon openly suffering individuals seeking and finding something that is actually quite rare and that they may not even know exists: evidence-based mental health care. It pains me to think about how poor those odds truly are.

My students and I, considering this problem and armed with the information I discussed in chapter 2 (i.e., ideation-to-action theories) proposed that the most important step we can take in suicide prevention is to implement broad scale prevention efforts focused entirely on the *capability* for suicide rather than the *desire* for suicide. Ideation-to-action theories such as the interpersonal theory of suicide (ITS) and three-step theory of suicide (3ST) posit that in order for people to engage in serious or lethal suicide attempts, they must not only desire death by suicide but also be capable of suicide. As discussed earlier, this variable consists of an elevated fearlessness about death and bodily harm, high levels of physiological pain tolerance, and sufficient access and comfort with highly lethal means. Individuals who desperately desire suicide but lack the capability are unlikely to transition from suicidal thoughts to suicidal behavior, and those with capability but no suicidal desire will only be at high risk for suicide if they develop suicidal thoughts in the future. When a person desires suicide and has the capability—a rather rare combination—risk skyrockets. If our treatments only target suicidal desire, we are missing an important opportunity to influence an equally powerful component of suicide risk: the extent to which an individual is capable of acting on thoughts of suicide. None of this is to say that we should ignore the agony of those suffering with suicidal desire but who lack the capability to transition from ideation to action. Instead, my proposed solutions highlight the importance of not exclusively focusing on desire.

In our paper, my students and I noted that suicide is not the first public health crisis in American history. As a nation, we have faced (and are still facing) many other threats to our health. Importantly though, the increasing rate of suicide stands in direct contrast to the trends of many other public health concerns, which is a good indicator that we are addressing those other concerns in ways that are lacking in our suicide prevention efforts. In an effort to learn from our successes in other areas, we considered American approaches to several public health problems, including HIV/AIDS and lung cancer and how our approaches to these problems are relevant to suicide prevention.

HIV/AIDS

On November 7, 1991, at the age of 32, basketball great Magic Johnson held a press conference to announce that he had been diagnosed as HIV positive and that he was retiring from the National Basketball Association immediately. I remember watching this press conference in stunned horror. I was less than two weeks shy of turning twelve years old, and all I knew about HIV was that it was deadly. And now there I was watching an athletic icon discussing what I assumed was a death sentence. As an avid sports fan, this was a severe disruption to my sense of the world. My assumptions were inaccurate, but they were not inexplicable at the time. We as a nation—at least those of us without MDs—knew very little about HIV in 1991, although most people probably knew more than I did at that point given that I was a child. The death rate associated with HIV and AIDS was still rising in the early 1990s and would peak in 1995 with a rate of 19.1 deaths per 100,000, more than 40% higher than the 2014 suicide rate.

At this point, I remember teachers occasionally mentioning HIV and AIDS to us in school and newscasters mentioning it as my family kept the news on during dinner, but I never heard any real messages of hope or detected any sense of optimism on the part of the individuals delivering the information. This seemed like a problem that would burden our society indefinitely going forward, even as many of those speaking about the illness claimed it only impacted specific subgroups of society, disparaging those subgroups in ways I did not quite realize was happening when I was a child. Our current status with the disease is thus likely well beyond the wildest hopes of Americans in the early 1990s, as the HIV/AIDS death rate is now 2.2 per 100,000.[2] The path from the emergence of the disease in the 1980s to its mortality peak in the mid-1990s to its current drastically reduced death rate is multifaceted, and I would not be doing anyone any favors by oversimplifying it. That being said, I believe there are several lessons we can learn from the successes in the fight against HIV/AIDS and apply to suicide prevention.

One component of this successful effort was a nationwide awareness and prevention campaign. In many locations, the distribution of free condoms increased, free and anonymous HIV testing was made available, and educational efforts were put into place to help individuals better understand how they can become vulnerable to

contracting the disease and what they can do to prevent that outcome. Research has shown that these campaigns were successful at
inspiring short-term behavioral changes but had minimal impact on
the actual mortality rate.[3]

Prevention efforts picked up more traction when they began to
focus on common means of contraction and specific methods for
rendering them less potent. Within the United States, intravenous
drug use (IDU) was the behavior that most commonly resulted in
new HIV infections.[4] Given this, it occurred to some that a potentially powerful method for reducing new HIV infections (and thus
lowering the HIV/AIDS death rate) would be to decrease the likelihood that IDU would result in infection. The most obvious method
for doing this would be to reduce IDU, an approach that parallels
abstinence-only approaches to the prevention of teenage pregnancy
and sexually transmitted diseases. If the risk behavior never occurs,
goes the logic, the negative outcome associated with that behavior
also will not occur. This point is indisputable on one level, but it is
severely weakened by the fact the people are typically not swayed to
stop doing what they want to do simply by being told it is dangerous and that they should stop. The history of humanity is flush with
examples of people making bad decisions even as somebody standing
next to them is telling them their plan is a bad idea. Given the unlike-
lihood of ridding the nation of IDU (if only!), prevention special-
ists chose the next best option: weakening the association between
IDU and HIV infection. Needle Exchange Programs (NEPs) became
more commonplace, where sterile injecting equipment was provided
to injecting drug users, along with referrals to health care and the
provision of legal and social services. Resistance to NEPs developed,
based on the fear that providing free equipment would increase IDU,
just as some fear sex education and the provision of free condoms
could increase teenage sexual behavior. As it turns out, however, this
approach not only did not increase needle sharing, it coincided with a
decrease in drug use among injecting drug users.[5,6,7] In contrast to the
fears of those who resisted this approach, needle sharing frequency
decreased following the implementation of NEPs and, importantly,
injecting drug users not using NEPs exhibited a 3.3-fold increase
in the risk of developing HIV relative to those using NEPs.[8] In one
study that compared cities with and without NEPs, scientists found
that injecting drug users in cities with NEPs exhibited a 5.7% annual

decrease in HIV infections as compared to a 5.9% annual *increase* in cities without NEPs.[9] Perhaps most astoundingly, HIV rates in the United States among injecting drug users have decreased by 80%.[10]

These numbers, though compelling, do not indicate that the NEPs are solely responsible for the drastically reduced HIV/AIDS death rate. There are many other factors that have played a role in that process, and it is not possible to precisely measure which approach had what degree of impact. Certainly the development and dissemination of antiretroviral therapy and other medications has been vital in preventing death among those diagnosed. What stands out for me with NEPs, however, is that they serve as a prevention approach capable of reaching groups larger than those who present at a clinic already showing symptoms of the disease. In a sense, by rendering needles less likely to cause infections, NEPs reduced injecting drug users' "capability" for HIV infection, just as my students and I have argued that we need to reduce the capability for suicide among the population at large (those with *and* without suicidal thoughts). Certainly, treating the drug-use behavior is as vitally important, just as treating suicidal thoughts remains important in a model that emphasizes treating suicidal capability. At the same time, by also addressing capability, the fight against HIV infections and HIV/AIDS deaths became substantially more effective, with a broader reach that prevented the onset of the illness rather than simply prolonging life among the infected. The parallel here is that we are currently in a good position, thanks to traditional mental health-care services, to help those who are already known to be in danger and who are seeking help. At the same time, those traditional approaches are not as effective as they could be if they reached high risk people who hide their suicidal thoughts and avoid mental health care. Reaching such individuals requires a prevention approach that makes prediction of risk less important by diminishing their ability to translate that risk into a lethal suicide attempt.

In suicide research, we refer to these sorts of approaches as "means safety." (Some use the phrase "means restriction," but the term "restriction" is off-putting to many, a finding confirmed not only by anecdotal evidence but also with compelling empirical research led by a doctoral student at Florida State University named Ian Stanley.[11]) "Means safety" refers to systematic efforts to increase the safe storage/use of tools that may be used in a suicide attempt or the (typically temporary) reduced access to those methods. With respect to HIV infections, means safety measures were reflected in efforts to take the item that most directly impacts new infections—a dirty needle—and render it less likely to cause the undesired outcome by replacing it with an inert alternative (a clean needle). Although reductions in drug use were noted in the research mentioned above, this is obviously not the most effective way to reduce that behavior. It does appear, however, to be an extremely effective method for reducing HIV infections and deaths. With respect to suicide risk, an optimal outcome would be complete resolution of all suicidal ideation. However, much like the elimination of IDU, this is not possible. So we are left to render thoughts of suicide less dangerous. Means safety represents our clearest path for doing so.

Lung Cancer

HIV/AIDS is not the only public health example worth considering as part of our suicide discussion. Another is the impressively successful (albeit far from complete) battle against lung cancer. Lung cancer remains an enormous problem in the United States. It is the leading cause of cancer death as well as the second most frequently diagnosed form of cancer. As troubling as those facts may seem, it is worth noting that the lung cancer incidence rate has decreased from 70 per 100,000 to 60 per 100,000, and the death rate has decreased from 60 per 100,000 to 50 per 100,000 since the early 1990s.[12] Indeed, in direct contrast to the national suicide rate, the rate of new lung cancer cases has decreased an average of 1.7% annually during the past decade.[13]

This reduction in rates of new lung cancer cases and deaths can be traced in many ways—although certainly not entirely—to changes in smoking patterns in the United States. Smoking is the leading cause of lung cancer, and smoking rates in the United States have decreased from 42.4% in 1965 to 17.8% in 2013. In other words, the most frequent method of disease contraction has become much rarer and, subsequently, the disease itself has become less common. Part of the shift in smoking behavior is likely associated with increased awareness of the association between smoking and lung cancer, a connection that was denied for an extended period before gaining mainstream acceptance. Increased knowledge alone does not explain these changes though. In addition, the presence of smoking in media representations has decreased dramatically, with characters on bill-boards, in print and TV ads, and on TV shows and in movies rarely smoking. Minors have seen reduced access to cigarettes, with more stringent ID checking at retail outlets. The price of cigarettes has increased dramatically and cigarette purchases have become more heavily taxed, thereby shifting the economic implications of the decision to buy a pack of cigarettes. Each of these shifts likely played a role in the decision of many people to quit (or not start) smoking. These approaches—aimed at reducing the behavior itself—stand in contrast to the HIV/AIDS approach in that NEPs did not truly aim to reduce drug use but rather break the association between needle usage and HIV infection. It should be noted, however, that age limits, ID checking, and financial penalties (through higher prices or increased taxes) all represent means safety efforts in a sense, as each render the acquisition of the method (cigarette) more difficult for at least certain portions of the population. A more similar approach in the fight against lung cancer can be seen in physical changes to the cigarette itself. Filters have become much more commonplace in an effort to reduce tar inhalation, and several low tar cigarettes have been marketed nationally.

Lessons Learned?

In each of these examples—HIV/AIDS and lung cancer—national or regional efforts at addressing the most common method of contracting the illness resulted in significant reductions in the occurrence of that illness. With respect to HIV/AIDS, this meant decreasing the extent to which dirty needles dominated the market by replacing them with clean needles; then utilizing those interactions with drug users to provide information regarding legal, medical, and social resources. The NEPs did not aim primarily to stop injecting drug use, although certainly health experts would have preferred that option. Instead, the individuals who led the implementation efforts aimed to decrease the frequency with which individuals contracted HIV by rendering needles less likely to cause infection. The implementation of these programs at the population level also sidestepped the issue of waiting for high-risk individuals to identify themselves and seek and optimally utilized effective health-care options. In doing so, they focused less on the known intentions of the individual and more on his or her capability to accomplish a specific and highly undesirable task: contracting HIV.

With respect to lung cancer, this meant making cigarettes harder to access—either through age limits and strict identification checks or through increased prices and taxation—and, to some extent, less potent through the increased use of filters. Here again, the method most commonly associated with causing the undesired outcome was not banned outright or fully removed from circulation. But efforts were made to decrease the likelihood that non-users become users or users contract lung cancer. Perhaps more than anything, the public tide against smoking changed dramatically. Strict limitations were implemented with respect to marketing in mass media (particularly with ads targeting children and other vulnerable populations). Limitations were also put into place in public places. I distinctly remember when smoking stopped being commonplace in airplanes and remain consciously thankful that armrest ashtrays (often full of a previous passengers' chewed gum leaking out of the sides and sticking to my shirt sleeve) are no longer standard. More recently, I remember the shifting tide against smoking in restaurants and bars. Just after college, I lived in Stamford, Connecticut for a few years and spent most weekends in New York City with friends. None of us were earning particularly large paychecks, so our nights often involved hanging out in an apartment or maybe seeing a movie. But sometimes we would wander from one restaurant or bar to another, listening to music, enjoying some drinks, and taking in the excitement of the vibrant city nightlife. Early on during that stretch, I would come home from a night out with friends, and my clothes would reek of cigarette smoke from other patrons. Febreze spray bottles were a staple in my apartment for this reason. In March 2003, however, the Smoke Free Air Act was implemented. Suddenly people who wanted to smoke while they were out with friends had to leave the restaurant or bar and huddle around an outdoor ashtray. My understanding of the rationale behind the law was to diminish the impact of second-hand smoke, but it also had ancillary benefits on the act of smoking itself. The law changed the value of smoking in one of the most popular contexts—while out socializing with friends—by forcing individuals to step away from their activities and peers, separating themselves (at times while entering cold or otherwise uncomfortable weather) specifically to engage in smoking. The incentives were thus shifted and the most common path to lung cancer became less traveled, at least for some.

The common thread between these two success stories is thus not one of a treatment for infected individuals but one of the use of a variety of methods to limit access to and decrease the potency of specific common methods for contracting dangerous illnesses. Another common thread however—and one I was highly aware of when selecting phenomena to compare to suicide—is stigma. With HIV/AIDS, many felt (and still feel) shame about their diagnoses and try to hide them. Worse yet, it took President Reagan several years to even say the name of the illness when it first started becoming a prominent issue in the 1980s, and the most high risk groups were openly disparaged and marginalized in response. Even as a child, I was aware of people speaking about HIV/AIDS as a "gay disease" or an illness for "junkies," with the focus of the conversation largely centered on belittling sexual minorities and those suffering from substance dependence, effectively blaming them for their own illness and drawing a line between "us" and "them."

What might surprise many readers is that this is not altogether different from the experiences of those diagnosed with cancer as recently as the mid- to late-20th century. As noted by Jimmie Holland and Jane Gooen-Piels,[14] the diagnosis of cancer was long thought to be a death sentence. Because of this, many practitioners did not reveal cancer diagnoses to patients, and many patients aware of their diagnoses hid the information from others. In the late 19th century, there were some emerging signs that some forms of cancer could be treatable: as a result, the American Cancer Society was formed. The American Cancer Society and other organizations worked to educate the public about the nature and treatability of various forms of cancer. It was not until the 1970s that practitioners began routinely revealing cancer diagnoses and those diagnosed began routinely disclosing their illnesses to others. This stands in stark contrast to where we are today, with pink ribbons adorning the jerseys of professional football players during Breast Cancer Awareness Month. Cancer survivors are now viewed—rightfully—as symbols of strength and hope, and support systems exist to help those just beginning the fight for their lives.

Individuals who suffered with HIV/AIDS or cancer at times when we were ineffective at prevention and treatment suffered shame, stigma, isolation, and hopelessness. This tragic situation is not altogether different from what many suicide attempt survivors and suicide loss survivors experience today. A first impulse might be to feel anger about the treatment of others in the past, but I would also encourage another response: one of hope. If we can turn the tide so effectively on other unspoken public health crises in this country, it seems perfectly reasonable to believe that we can do the same with suicide. With HIV/AIDS and lung cancer, means safety was a vital component of the shifting tide. With lung cancer, such efforts required overcoming powerful lobbyists and a remarkable resistance to scientific evidence. Suicide prevention efforts focused on guns will require a similar achievement. I would argue that the lessons learned from our national successes with HIV/AIDS and lung cancer can be applied to suicide, with a particular emphasis on guns. Fortunately, my case for this argument is not purely theoretical, as a robust research base exists for the utility of means safety with other suicide methods.

Means Safety and Suicide

Renowned poet and author Sylvia Plath chronicled her struggle with depression and a nonlethal suicide attempt in her 1963 novel, *The Bell Jar*. She rose to fame when she was quite young—only in her twenties—and as she and her husband, the poet Ted Hughes, were raising two small children. On February 11, 1963, again battling depression and now separated from her husband after his infidelity, Sylvia Plath died by suicide while her two children slept in her London home. Plath died as a result of the inhalation of toxic gas after putting her head into her oven. As noted by Norman Kreitman in a highly cited study from 1976,[15] this was the most common method of death by suicide in the United Kingdom in the late 1950s and 1960s. At that time, domestic gas in the United Kingdom was toxic, comprising 10% to 20% carbon monoxide.

Beginning in 1958, the United Kingdom gradually introduced natural gas that was largely detoxified, and by the early 1970s, the vast majority of natural gas used within the United Kingdom was nontoxic. Impressively, that same period was marked by a steep

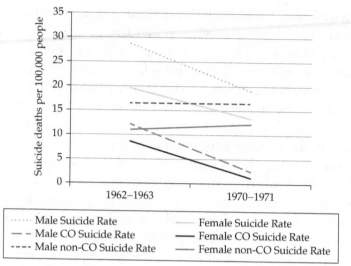

FIGURE 5.1 Changes in Suicide Rates in England and Wales Following the Detoxification of Gas.

Source: Kreitman, N. (1976). The coal gas story. United Kingdom suicide rates, 1960-71. *British Journal of Preventative and Social Medicine, 30,* 86–93.

decrease in suicides (see Figure 5.1). As noted in Kreitman's paper, the suicide rate among men in England and Wales decreased from 28.7 per 100,000 in 1962–1963 to 19.0 per 100,000 in 1970–1971 (33.8% decrease). For women, the rate during that period decreased from 19.6 per 100,000 to 13.3 per 100,000 (38.0% decrease). These decreases in overall suicide rates can largely be accounted for by dramatic drops in suicides by carbon monoxide poisoning, which was what actually killed people who used gas ovens as their means of suicide. In men, the rate by that specific method decreased from 12.2 per 100,000 to 2.4 per 100,000 (80.3% decrease), while the suicide rate by other methods remained stable (16.5 per 100,000 in 1962–1963 to 16.6 per 100,000 in 1970–1971). In women, the rate by that specific method decreased from 8.6 per 100,000 to 1.1 per 100,000 (87.2% decrease), with only a minimal rise in suicides by other methods (11.0 per 100,000 in 1962–1963 to 12.2 per 100,000 in 1970–1971). By removing the toxicity of an otherwise highly lethal and frequently used method for suicide through a population-level prevention approach, the United Kingdom was able to save many thousands of lives.

Impressive on its own, this is far from the only example of means safety as an effective suicide prevention tool. Another prominent example is the bridge barrier. As I noted in Chapter 3, falling is a relatively rare suicide method in the United States, with only 2.3% of all suicide deaths in 2014 classified as resulting from falls. The fatality of the method is more variable than it is for many others because it depends on a variety of factors (e.g., height of the jump, the nature of the landing spot), but the calculations I reported earlier indicate that around one in four jumps intended to cause harm result in death. Because falling accounts for such a small percentage of suicide deaths, any prevention effort specific to jumping would likely have minimal impact on the overall suicide rate, but a life saved is a life saved, and the research in this area has obvious relevance to suicide prevention across methods.

With respect to bridges, prevention efforts have largely centered on the construction of barriers, which could consist of high fences curved inward at the top, large nets to catch those who jump, or several other designs. Given that the number of jumping deaths is low and that researchers cannot experimentally manipulate the presence or absence of bridge barriers, this phenomenon is somewhat difficult to study, but many scientists have nonetheless reported rather impressive findings. For instance, one study published in the *British Journal of Psychiatry* focused on the Clifton Suspension Bridge in Bristol, England.[16] In 1998 officials installed a barrier on this bridge, and the authors of this study examined jumping deaths from the bridge in the years preceding (1994–1998) and following (1999–2003) the barrier's installation. In the years leading up to the construction of the barrier, a yearly average of 8.2 individuals died by suicide after jumping from this bridge. In the years following its installation, however, that number dropped to 4.0. Nearly all of the deaths were by men, but the authors of the study noted that there was no evidence that male jumping deaths increased at any other sites, a point I will return to in chapter 8.

A similar story can be told by a study published by Anna Beautrais and colleagues in 2009.[17] The authors examined patterns of suicides resulting from jumps at the Grafton Bridge in Auckland, New Zealand. For 60 years, the bridge had featured barriers to prevent suicide. In 1996, however, the barriers were removed. In the years leading up to the removal (1991–1996), there were five suicide deaths from jumping off the bridge (one per year). During the period 1997–2002, however, after the barrier was removed, that figure was 19 (3.17 per year). In response to this surge, officials re-installed barriers in early 2003, this time with an improved design. In the subsequent years (2003–2006), there were no deaths from jumping from the bridge, nor was there any evidence of increased suicides by jumping at other local bridges. This story reinforces the notion that installing bridge barriers can be helpful but also emphasizes that the removal of means safety measures can on its own prompt a rise in deaths by suicide.

A "suicide hotspot" is a specific location at which many suicides occur relative to other locations. In the United States the most prominent example is the Golden Gate Bridge, but many others exist worldwide. Researchers in Australia studied two local bridge hotspots over the course of several years,[18] the Gateway and Story bridges in Brisbane, which accounted for nearly half (45.5%) of all suicides by jumping in Brisbane between 1990 and 2012. In 1993 officials installed a barrier on the Gateway Bridge, and as you might expect from the studies I described above, the number of suicides at that bridge dropped by 53% in the years following the installation (1994–1997) relative to the preceding years (1990–1993). Just as importantly, however, there was no evidence that individuals thwarted in an effort to use one hotspot (Gateway) opted instead to jump from the other (Story).

These findings are consistent with a review published by Jane Pirkis and colleagues in 2015 in the prestigious journal *Lancet Psychiatry*.[19] The authors examined 18 different studies of prevention efforts centered on suicide at specific hotspots, focusing on three specific categories of suicide prevention: environments that increase the likelihood of intervention by a third party (e.g., bridges with high levels of foot traffic), interventions that encourage help-seeking (e.g., signs prominently displaying suicide hotline information), and interventions that restrict access to lethal means (e.g., bridge barriers). Pirkis and her colleagues found that all three types of preventions were helpful but that restricting access to lethal means was by far the most effective, reducing suicides at hotspots by over 90%.

Taken together, the findings related to the detoxification of natural gas in the United Kingdom and to the installation of bridge barriers at suicide hotspots provide robust evidence that the lessons learned in the reduction of deaths by HIV/AIDS and lung cancer can be effectively applied to suicide. What strikes me about this is the simplicity of it. Suicide is hard. When you make highly lethal and commonly used methods for suicide harder to use or less effective in causing death, fewer people die. Much more difficult to understand, in my view, is why means safety techniques are not discussed more often and implemented more broadly.

There exists another simple and intuitively appealing way to further reduce the number of deaths by suicide in this country. Tens of thousands of American lives could be saved every year with a few reasonable and inexpensive steps. The next two chapters will explore the evidence supporting gun-related means safety efforts. Some of these may be less than palatable to many gun owners, but the lessons learned from research on bridge barriers and carbon monoxide deaths in the United Kingdom cannot be ignored when it comes to guns.

Legislating Means Safety
Measures for Guns

The purpose of government is to enable the people of a nation to live in safety and happiness. Government exists for the interest of the governed, not for the governors.

—Thomas Jefferson

The duty of a patriot is to protect his country from its government.

—Thomas Paine

I AM A STAUNCHLY LIBERAL NONRELIGIOUS MAN FROM THE northeast who lives in Mississippi, and as I am writing this, a new presidential administration has deepened the political divide between left and right. On a daily basis I witness a range of strong opinions regarding the worth and role of government as articulated in local and national media. Growing up, my general sense of the government was that it was there to help us and to develop and maintain a system of rules enabling our country to function properly. Being a fairly rule-bound child, I saw this as not unlike life at school, where there were certainly rules that I did not like or agree with, but where I generally felt like the system existed to keep me and my friends safe and to help us learn. As I grew into an adult, my sense of the government as magnanimous, and my understanding of the individuals we elect to higher offices, have evolved. But I still generally land in the camp that sees the government as a vehicle through which to guide positive behavior changes within the nation. I do acknowledge some limits to this, but from a public health perspective I have typically seen a lot of value in the government (federal, state, and local) implementing policies that encourage healthy behavior and discourage dangerous and unhealthy ones.

This chapter, however, is not about the value of government. You and I need not agree on politics in general in order for an informed conversation to develop regarding legislative efforts to address suicide.

In chapter 5 I explained the concept of means safety. I discussed how means safety has played a role in diminishing the impact of diseases such as HIV/AIDS and lung cancer and then linked that to efforts to address nonfirearm suicides. Considering the entirety of that evidence base, I would argue that the power of means safety in reducing disease burden and death is undeniable. So the question here is not *whether* means safety would be useful in addressing firearm suicides (and thus suicides in general), but *how*. This chapter and the next will explore two options, the second of which—nonlegislative approaches—will likely be seen as uncontroversial by most readers. The first option, however, focuses on the use of means safety legislation and is likely to stir some debate.

This chapter is part history lesson—it is the story of firearm legislation and varying opinions about its impact over time. And as is the case with any history lesson, it is important to consider who is telling the story. Throughout these pages I have been forthcoming about my own political leanings and personal feelings about guns, but I am hopeful that those who do not share my opinions nevertheless feel that I have been fair in my presentation, which relies on evidence rather than opinion. Some may read this chapter and conclude that I have deviated from that practice, so I want to open the discussion with a disclosure of my general views on this aspect of suicide prevention. Then I will walk you through its history.

I hold that legislative solutions are an important aspect of suicide prevention, but they are only one aspect. I believe that they are likely extremely powerful tools for addressing certain components of the problem (such as preventing high-risk individuals from acquiring guns in the first place) and less useful for others (such as regulating the behavior of people who already own guns). The truest test of the utility of legislation would be a study examining the effects of specific laws in states with high gun ownership rates and high suicide rates; however, such states tend not to support laws regulating gun ownership, so it is difficult to know exactly how they would play out in those contexts.

You need not take my word on any of this: I urge readers to consider the evidence and make informed decisions on their own. To facilitate this I will summarize the successes and failures related to legislation and suicide since the mid-20th century. An important point to keep in mind, however—and I touched on this in the introduction to the book—is that Congress has prevented the CDC from funding gun violence–related research for more than 20 years. I believe the research being done nevertheless on this topic is strong and that it paints a fairly clear picture. However, when considered within the context of an environment in which research is being actively suppressed, my interpretation is that if anything we are most likely underestimating the importance of laws in gun suicide prevention. That is obviously conjecture, but not, I think, without merit.

Early Research on Firearm Legislation and Suicide

When considering early work on firearm legislation and suicide, it is important to keep the larger context in mind with respect to gun ownership. For example, firearm ownership increased dramatically during the mid- to late 20th century, a shift that coincided with a national firearm suicide rate that increased from 4.9 per 100,000 in 1953 to 7.1 in 1978. During that same time period, the nonfirearm suicide rate remained flat, indicating that increases in suicide rates overall were almost entirely due to a surge in Americans killing themselves with guns.[1]

In the early 1980s, a researcher named David Lester began publishing a series of studies examining the potential role of firearms legislation in suicide prevention. Across several studies, he demonstrated that states with more restrictive gun laws exhibited lower statewide suicide rates, with data drawn from as early as 1960 and as recent as the late 1980s.[2,3,4] An important critique of these studies, however, was that none of them controlled for the effects of other variables. In other words, Lester did not consider the relationship between other variables (such as age, gender, and socioeconomic status) and whether suicide rates could be explained by them. When a study fails to control for other variables the argument can be made that one or more of those other variables may better explain its results. Scientists can never fully eliminate that concern—there is always something else we could have measured—but we can increase confidence in our results quite a bit when they show a unique effect for a specific variable above and beyond the effect of others. Beginning in the late 1980s David Lester and other researchers started taking that point to heart, although in the beginning admittedly with fairly short lists of "other variables." For instance, in a study published in 1987, Lester reported that strict gun laws predicted state suicide rates even after accounting for the effects of church attendance[5], a behavior previously shown to be protective against suicide (due to social connection, however, not due to stigmatizing beliefs about the eternal fate of suicide decedents).

A few years later, Myron Boor and Jeffrey Bair of Emporia State University took this a step further. Building on work by Lester that had demonstrated that laws governing the buying and selling of handguns are more powerful in suicide prevention than are laws governing carriers of handguns, Boor and Bair found that handgun laws restricting buyers and sellers of handguns were associated with significantly lower statewide suicide rates in 1985, even after controlling for sex differences, age, race, population density, the percentage of the population living in a metropolitan area, the divorce rate, the crime rate, and the unemployment rate. This study provides evidence that particular types of laws might matter more than others and that these effects are not better explained by certain other variables known to be associated with suicide.

These early studies were conducted at the national level, but others approached the issue locally. One such group of studies came about thanks to the Firearms Control Regulations Act (FCRA), which was signed into law in Washington, DC, on July 23, 1976, six days before David "Son of Sam" Berkowitz shot his first victim. The law went into effect on September 24, 1976, three weeks after Australia banned all radio and television advertising for cigarettes and tobacco, a truly massive means safety effort. The FCRA represented a pronounced effort on the part of the city of Washington to diminish gun ownership. The possession of handguns was essentially banned for everyone other than law enforcement officers. Anyone else who wanted to own a handgun (or any other firearm) had to register the weapon unless he or she had already registered it prior to the implementation of the law. Automatic weapons and high-capacity semi-automatic weapons were banned entirely. New rifle and shotgun purchases were limited to specific officially licensed dealers and the buyers had to meet specifications regarding age, criminal record, physical fitness, and knowledge of firearm laws and safety. All privately owned weapons were required to be stored unloaded, disassembled, and secured (with a trigger lock, for instance) unless they were actively being used for legal recreational purposes such as hunting or if they were stored in a place of business.

The fact that the FCRA was implemented in only one city hinders our ability to understand its broader utility as a suicide prevention tool, but this does not prevent any examination of its impact. To this end, in 1991 Colin Loftin of the University of Maryland and several of his colleagues published a study in the *New England Journal of Medicine*[6] examining shifts in homicide and suicide rates in DC following the implementation of the FCRA. In this study, the authors looked at both firearm homicides and firearm suicides between 1968 and 1987 and found that rates of both behaviors declined by approximately 25% during the period following the implementation of the FCRA. There was a slight increase in both homicides and suicides by nonfirearm methods during that same time period but not nearly enough to offset the decrease in gun-related deaths. The authors also looked at homicide and suicide rates in adjacent areas and found no changes there, so the downward shift in suicides in DC did not simply mirror a broader trend in a larger geographic area; instead it represented a shift in the discrete area directly affected by the law.

On June 6, 2008, the United States Supreme Court overturned several portions of this law in the *District of Columbia v. Heller*. In that ruling, it was determined that gun lock requirements and a ban on handgun ownership both violated the Second Amendment. Registration requirements and an assault weapon ban remain, but the other components of the law have been repealed. To be fair, the effect of the repeal of the law on suicide rates in DC is not clear. In the years leading up to the repeal (1999–2007), the suicide rate ranged from 4.02 to 6.96 per 100,000. In the years following the repeal (2008–2014), the rate has ranged from 4.90 to 7.89 per 100,000. The numbers are higher post-2008, but given that the national suicide rate has climbed each year during that span, it is difficult to interpret that finding in isolation.

Although I will examine this point in greater detail in chapter 8, it is worth noting that in 1990 a study was published in the *American Journal of Psychiatry* reporting that declines in firearm suicide rates following the implementation of firearm legislation were offset by suicides by falling.[7] This understandably created a bit of a stir—after all, the goal of suicide prevention is to prevent suicide, not to change the way it happens. As it turns out though, other scientists skeptical of this finding (jumping accounts for well below 10% of annual suicides whereas firearms account for 50%), reanalyzed those same data using a longer time frame, and their results negated the claim of the original authors.[8] Suicides by other methods did not offset gains made through a decline in firearm suicides.

More Recent Research on Firearm Legislation and Suicide

Beyond the early to mid-1990s, there was a lull in research on firearm legislation and suicide, but in the early 2000s it began to pick up again. This new wave of studies generally took one of two approaches: considering laws in general or focusing specifically on laws relevant to the Brady Handgun Violence Prevention Act.

In 2003 Ken Conner and Yueying Zhong published a study in the *American Journal of Preventative Medicine*[9] looking at firearm laws and statewide suicide rates. These authors divided states into groups they considered as having restrictive laws (eight states), modest laws (22 states), and unrestrictive laws (20 states). Controlling for the effects of race, income, and urbanization, these authors found that stricter gun laws were associated with lower suicide rates. Given that men have higher suicide rates and are more likely to use a gun in a suicide attempt, the authors also thought it might be important to test the extent to which this was true for both men and women. As it turns out, despite sex differences in rates of overall and firearm suicides, the model held for both men and women.

The next year, James Price and Amy Thompson of Mississippi State University and Joseph Dake of Wayne State University published a study in the *Journal of Community Health*[10] that was not as unambiguously supportive of the utility of firearm legislation in preventing suicide. The authors found that firearm suicide rates were particularly closely associated with firearm prevalence but were also associated with firearm laws. This point was true whether laws were considered in isolation (laws were broken down into categories of crime deterrence, government control, possession, safety, and sales restriction) or in combination (all laws considered together). Things became more complicated, however, when the authors considered gun laws, firearm prevalence, and a host of other variables (alcohol consumption, urbanization, violent crime rate, poverty, unemployment, education) at the same time. In those analyses, gun prevalence was still significantly associated with suicide rates, but gun laws were not. Such a finding points to the simple presence of a gun as a factor more important than the law itself. You will notice as I describe more studies from this same time period and beyond, however, that this pattern of results is not constant across studies. Furthermore, if gun laws impact rates of gun ownership, it would make sense that controlling for gun ownership wipes out the effects of the laws in a statistical analysis. To put this in plainer terms, consider the following scenario. If I am in a bad mood in the middle of the afternoon and I eat a snack, my mood often improves. Considering this statistically, we could see that the consumption of snacks is associated with an improvement in mood. If I controlled for changes in hunger level, however, the relationship between snack eating and mood would likely disappear. This is because the mechanism through which snacking helps moods (at least sometimes) is the elimination of hunger. This does not mean that snacking was not vital or useful—it simply means that snacking is one way to get rid of hunger, which in turn can help your mood. Returning to the guns example, if gun prevalence wipes out the effect of gun laws on suicide rates (which it does not always do), this does not mean that gun laws are irrelevant or not useful—it could simply mean that gun laws diminish gun prevalence, which in turn reduces suicide rates. The fact that we understand how the law might work does not make the law less useful. On the contrary, it highlights why legislation might have such potential as a broad suicide prevention tool.

This point was made in a more recent study by Eric Fleegler, Lots Lee, Michael Monuteaux, David Hemenway, and Rebekah Mantix, published in 2013 in *JAMA Internal Medicine*.[11] Examining data from 2007 through 2010, the authors controlled for the effects of race, sex, poverty, unemployment, college education, population density, and firearm ownership (using the proportion of suicides resulting from firearms as a proxy for firearm ownership). States were rated on the strength of their gun laws using two methods. The first involved simply adding up the number of gun laws present in a given state. The second involved weighing some laws more heavily than others, based upon the opinion of the Brady Center to Prevent Gun Violence[12] regarding the relevance of specific laws to gun violence. Regardless of which scoring method was used, states with higher gun law scores exhibited lower suicide rates. This effect, however, was attenuated when the authors also controlled for gun ownership. Here again, we see a situation in which gun ownership rates seem to explain the relationship between at least some gun laws and state-level suicide rates. I view this as a partial explanation for why the gun laws might work and others view it as a sign that the laws themselves are not our best path forward. My counter to the latter view is simply a question: if laws are dismissed because gun ownership is the real issue, what is the alternate proposal for diminishing gun ownership?

Before turning to a discussion of the Brady law, I want to discuss one more study. In 2011 Antonio Rodriguez Andres and Katherine Hempstead published research in *Health Policy* that examined state firearm regulations and suicide in the years 1995 to 2004. In some ways, this study was similar to others I have discussed. Here, the authors found that more restrictive laws were associated with lower male suicide rates, even after controlling for income, unemployment, alcohol consumption, and the percentage of the population aged 65 and older. What stands out about this study, however, is that the results indicated that laws limiting gun access more generally had a stronger association with suicide rates than did laws that targeted specific populations, based either on criminal history or on behavioral problems associated with suicide risk. The implications here are substantial, and they mirror what I discussed in chapter 4. On an intuitive level, it makes sense to focus our attention on "high risk" populations. For one thing, despite its status as the tenth leading cause of death in the country, suicide is a relatively rare outcome. So when we can narrow the population down, our odds of predicting it would in theory go up. This is one of the fundamental principles of suicide risk assessments. Taking this a step further, it also seems potentially more pragmatic to develop laws in this manner so as to reduce the risk that gun owners will interpret the law as a broad assault on constitutional rights. The funny thing about science, however, is that the results sometimes obliterate our intuition. When we narrow laws to "high risk" individuals, the impact of the law diminishes. Remember that one of the issues I raised in chapter 4 was that some of the groups most likely to use a gun in a suicide attempt—men in general, middle-aged and older adult males, in particular, soldiers—have a tendency to avoid mental health care altogether and to deny suicidal ideation even when they are experiencing thoughts of suicide. Because of this, it is actually difficult to identify "high risk" individuals on a case-by-case basis before the death occurs, so laws designed to focus gun access regulations on those most at risk of using a gun in a suicide attempt are still likely to overlook a certain number of people at risk for suicide. But laws that impact population-level gun access would have an impact on high-risk individuals regardless of whether they are so identified.

Perhaps it is not unreasonable to argue that it is unfair to burden everyone with restrictive laws when only a few individuals are in need of intervention. I am not entirely unsympathetic to this—it is frustrating to be required to take precautions when we perceive no risk—but the stakes here are so high and the intervention so minimal that the inconvenience (if any even exists) seems to me an acceptable price for saving potentially thousands of lives each year. I will touch on the nature of this perceived inconvenience toward the end of the chapter, but before doing so I want to discuss one more set of studies: those focused on the Brady Law.

On November 30, 1993—one week before Colin Ferguson fatally shot six people and injured another 19 on a Long Island Railroad train—President Bill Clinton signed the Brady Handgun Violence Prevention Act into law. The law, which went into effect in February 1994, required federal background checks and a five-day waiting period prior to all firearm sales in the United States. In 1998, with the creation of the National Instant Criminal Background Check System (NICS), the waiting period requirement was removed, as the NICS check can often be completed in a matter of seconds over the phone as the dealer is completing a transaction with a gun buyer.

Given the difficulty of passing federal laws related to firearms and the law's stated goal of reducing gun violence, it should be unsurprising that several researchers have since studied the impact of the legislation on gun deaths. With respect to suicide, the first influential study published on the topic appeared in the *Journal of the American Medical Association*[13] (JAMA) in 2000, written by Jens Ludwig and Phillip Cook. To assess the impact of the law, the authors examined homicide and suicide rates from 1985 through 1997 and controlled for the effects of age, race, poverty, income, urban residence, and alcohol consumption. Prior to the implementation of the Brady Law, 18 states already had background check and waiting period legislation in place and, as such, the authors were able to compare 32 "treatment sites" (states that implemented background check and waiting period systems in response to the Brady Law) to 18 "control sites" that did not need to change in order to be in compliance with the law. Their results were not particularly supportive of the Brady Law as a prominent force in the prevention of violent deaths. The only analysis in which they saw a significant difference was in firearm suicides among individuals aged 55 and above. In that demographic group, the states that changed their laws in response to the Brady Law saw a steeper decline in suicide deaths than did states with such laws in place prior to the implementation of the law. The authors also noted that results in general were significantly stronger in states that had to change both background check and waiting period laws than in states that only needed to change one in order to be in compliance.

In some ways, this appears to argue against the Brady Law as particularly effective. Recently, however, Steven Sumner, Peter Layde, and Clare Guse of the Medical College of Wisconsin published a rebuttal of sorts in the *Journal of Preventative Medicine*.[14] The authors noted that just because a law is in place across states does not mean that the law is followed in the same way and with equal effectiveness in each state. With background checks, for instance, some states rely upon federal checks, some rely upon state-level checks, and some use more local checks through municipal police or sheriff offices. All background checks utilize the NICS system, but more local checks are also sometimes able to draw upon data not available at the federal level. The authors also noted that of the over eight million applications for gun sales in 2004, only 126,000 (1.6%) were actually rejected, meaning that background checks are not actually systematically preventing many people from buying guns. This ties in well with my earlier assertion that the inconvenience of firearm laws (a background check lasting a matter of seconds that does not prevent the acquisition of a gun in 98.4% of cases) is likely overstated and based more on a broader philosophy on gun control than an actual response to a difficult situation.

In this study, Summer and his colleagues looked at data from 2002 through 2004, well after the implementation of the Brady Law, and considered only individuals aged 21 and older, as any gun sale to an individual below that age would be considered illegal according to the law. In their analyses, the authors controlled for unemployment, robbery rate, income inequality level, poverty, alcohol consumption, urban population, divorce rate, age, and race. Based on their understanding of the manner in which background checks were processed in each state during this time period, they categorized 21 states as relying solely upon federal background checks, 17 as supplementing federal checks with state-level information, and 12 states as supplementing federal checks with more localized information. They found that more local levels for background checks were associated with lower state firearm suicide rates—11.64 per 100,000 for federal-level checks, 8.45 per 100,000 for state-level checks, and 5.74 per 100,000 for local-level checks. This pattern was true across all age groups. When the authors ran multivariate analyses, which means they considered all of their covariates at the same time as their predictor (how local the background check system was in each state), they found that states using local level background checks had 27% lower firearm suicide rates than did states using only federal background checks. The authors of this study noted that background checks are fairly easily thwarted, particularly when no local information is considered. Because of this, the utility of a law can only truly be determined when we factor in the extent to which the law is being implemented effectively. A reasonable response might be that a law that inspires such inconsistent quality of implementation is not ideal, and I would not disagree; however, such a conclusion does not in any way discount the utility of background checks—it simply highlights the need for greater specificity in the writing of the law and the importance of emphasizing interventions and legislation alongside evidence that they are associated with the desired outcome (in this case, lower suicide rates).

Research From the Anestis Lab

I began my scientific foray into firearms one hot day in the spring of 2014. Feeling out of place in my current home state—a state of deep economic and social conservatism and an area awash in guns—I started extracting all of the data I could find relevant to guns and suicide and considering how I could bring a scientific perspective to an emotional argument. As a suicide researcher, I was already aware of some of the information I have discussed throughout this book, but I was still a newcomer to this particular aspect of suicide prevention. That day marked the beginning of a line of research in my lab that has continuously gained momentum over the past several years. My first step was to open an empty file on SPSS, the statistical software I tend to use when running analyses. It looks a lot like Microsoft Excel but allows some more advanced statistical work that is common in psychological research. I then opened the CDC's WISQARS website, which tracks violent injuries and deaths on the state and national level, and started entering overall and firearm suicide rates for every state for 2010. That task did not take particularly long, but I was not finished: I also needed information on guns themselves and, in this case, I was interested in laws.

Given my acute sense of being an outsider—a feeling that was particularly salient that day—I wanted to be careful in how I approached this task. The purpose of science is not to advance an agenda or to prove that one's own philosophies are superior. The purpose of science is to be skeptical of our own sense of truth and to test our ideas to see if they truly map on to the world as it exists in reality. No matter how thoroughly we attempt to abide by this idea, however, the appearance of an agenda can often prompt others to dismiss our work as political.

This left me with a bit of a dilemma. How could I decide objectively which gun laws to consider? How not to look as though I were putting my finger on the scale, intentionally influencing my results to advance a cause? I spent an hour or so pondering this before arriving at a clear answer—I decided simply to let the gun lobby pick the laws for me. The National Rifle Association's Institute for Legislative

Action (NRA-ILA) maintains a website that tracks gun-related laws on a state-by-state basis.[15] My thought here was that nobody could accuse me of cherry picking laws if the most prominent gun lobbying organization was already tracking the laws I chose. Given that handguns account for a large proportion of firearm suicides, I restricted my search to state laws related to handguns and, given what the NRA-ILA was tracking, the best options seemed to be laws requiring (1) a permit to purchase handguns (2) the registration of handguns and (3) the licensing of handgun owners. I also had members of my research team track down whether any states had changed (implemented or repealed) any of these laws in the years leading up to the most recently available suicide data.

The results of this study, published in the influential *American Journal of Public Health* in 2015,[16] were entirely consistent with my expectations. In this paper, we considered a number of questions. The first was whether states in which a higher proportion of suicide deaths result from guns account for a disproportionate amount of U.S. suicides. To do this, we compared the nine states with the lowest proportion of suicides due to guns to the nine states with the highest proportion of suicides resulting from guns. The nine states (we counted the District of Columbia too) with the lowest proportion— Hawaii (18%), Massachusetts (23%), Rhode Island (23%), New Jersey (26%), New York (30%), Connecticut (31%), DC (32%), Illinois (38%), and California (38%)—accounted for just over 91 million people, or 29.5% of the 2010 US population. Those same states accounted for 22.6% of US suicides overall. Had each of those nine states had a suicide rate that matched the 2010 national suicide rate (12.43 per 100,000), we would have expected an additional 2,643 suicide deaths in those states than we actually saw.

In comparison, the nine states with the highest proportion of suicides resulting from guns—West Virginia (75%), Louisiana (69%), Alabama (67%), Mississippi (66%), Alaska (65%), Kentucky (64%), Georgia (63%), Wyoming (63%), and Idaho (63%)—accounted for just over 31 million people, or 10.0% of the 2010 U.S. population. In contrast, they accounted for 11.1% of all U.S. suicides. Had each of these states had a suicide rate consistent with the national rate in 2010, we would have expected 134 fewer deaths. This might seem like a negligible difference, but let me use raw numbers to explain why it was not. Despite that fact that the first list of nine states had

60 million more people in 2010, there were only 4,400 more suicides in those states—and only 130 more firearm suicides. A difference of 130 firearm suicides between groups that differ in population by 60 million people is astounding.

Our next task was to find out whether each of the three laws we were examining were associated with lower overall suicide rates, firearm suicide rates, and percentage of suicides resulting from firearms. In these analyses, we controlled for the effects of poverty and population density. For both permit and license laws, states with the laws in place had lower overall and firearm suicide rates and a lower percentage of suicides resulting in firearms. Specifically, the 14 states with permit laws had an overall suicide rate of 10.3 per 100,000 (15.5 for those without) and a firearm suicide rate of 4.0 per 100,000 (8.8 for those without), with 38% of all suicides resulting from guns (56% in states without). The 14 states with license laws had an overall suicide rate of 11.2 per 100,000 (15.2 for those without) and a firearms suicide rate of 5.3 per 100,000 (8.3 for those without), with 43% of suicides resulting from guns (54% for those without). For registration laws, results were only statistically significant for firearm suicide rates and the percentage of suicides resulting from firearms. The seven states with registration laws in place had an overall suicide rate of 11.0 per 100,000 (14.6 for those without) and a firearms suicide rate of 4.3 per 100,000 (8.0 for those without), with 38% of suicides resulting from firearms (53% for those without).

Simply noticing some difference between two groups does not tell you much about why that difference exists. In this case, we noticed a difference in suicide rates between states with and without specific gun laws in place, but we wanted to better understand why those differences exist. One assumption we had was that, when such laws are in place, guns are less often the method of choice in suicide deaths and, because this particularly lethal method is less common, the overall suicide rates would be lower. This is a test of indirect effects—an idea I discussed earlier in the book when I talked about how taller people are more likely to be bald, but only because taller people are more likely to be men. Our analyses on this point were largely consistent with our expectations, which we took to mean one or more of three possibilities: in states with such laws in place, people attempt suicide less often, people attempt suicide using less lethal means and therefore survive at a higher rate, and people simply own fewer guns.

The last point we considered was whether changes in these laws coincided with changes in suicide rates, a question that was the focus of much of the research on the FCRA and the Brady Law. There were few changes to these particular laws during the time period for which we had data, so we could not run traditional statistical tests. What we did instead was simply report trends in the two states that implemented licensing laws—Maryland and California implemented them in 2003—leading up to and following implementation. Both states—and the United States overall—reported an increase in the suicide rate in the years leading up to the implementation of the law (2001–2003). What stands out, however, is that whereas the nation as a whole saw a continued increase in the suicide rate from 2003–2006 (2.9% increase), both California (3.9% decrease) and Maryland (4.8% decrease) saw their rates go down. Could these shifts be considered entirely accounted for by the laws? Certainly not, but when these results are considered alongside the rest of the results from our paper, the overall picture is clear.

A year later, my wife and colleague Joye Anestis and I decided to follow up on this paper and take it a step further. I think my decision to focus on NRA-ILA laws to negate concerns of bias was a good one, but the result was that we focused on laws that did not seem as relevant to suicide prevention as others might be. Remember that David Klonsky promotes the idea that access to and comfort with lethal means is a vital component of the capability for suicide. Given this, we thought the most relevant laws would be ones that are directly related to access and exposure to handguns. Along these lines, we opted to examine universal background checks, mandatory waiting periods, the requirement that gun locks be used in at least some circumstances, and the restriction of the open carrying of handguns. Here again, our results were published in 2015 in the *American Journal of Public Health* (actually, the two studies were published next to one another in the same issue).[17]

In this second study, we improved on the first one in several ways. First, as I already mentioned, we picked laws that we believed had more relevance to suicide prevention. Second, we used more recent data, reflecting the most current data at the time (2013). Third, we added more variables into the equation to help further rule out that other important ideas might better account for our findings. This list included poverty, education, race/ethnicity, age, and population density. We also consulted with the Law Center to Prevent Gun Violence, and staff there agreed to share a database with us detailing changes in law status across states dating back to 2009.

The results in this study paralleled those from the first one quite closely. For each of the four laws, the firearm suicide rate and percentage of suicides resulting from firearms were lower in states with the law in place. For each law other than the one governing waiting periods, the overall suicide rate was lower as well. With respect to waiting periods, the overall rate was lower before we accounted for other factors (e.g., age, poverty) but became non-significant once we entered those variables into the equation. We should note, however, that the effect size was a medium effect here. Statistical significance depends upon how large your sample is and 51 (the states plus DC) is a small sample, which makes it hard to find "significant" results, especially when you are entering a lot of variables into the equation like we did. Effect sizes do not depend upon sample sizes and medium-sized effects are important, so I would be cautious in dismissing the waiting period results.

To add more specificity to that previous paragraph, the 11 states with waiting periods had an overall suicide rate of 11.45 per 100,000 (15.72 for those without) and a firearm suicide rate of 4.43 per 100,000 (8.98 for those without), with 35.8% of all suicide resulting from guns (55.8% for those without). The 17 states with background checks had an overall suicide rate of 11.42 per 100,000 (16.49 for those without) and a firearm suicide rate of 4.53 per 100,000 (9.74 for those without), with 36.8% of all suicides resulting from guns (58.8% for those without). The 20 states that restricted open carrying of handguns had an overall suicide rate of 12.16 per 100,000 (16.50 for those without) and a firearm suicide rate of 5.58 per 100,000 (9.56 for those without), with 42.1% of all suicides resulting from guns (57.5% for those without). Lastly, the four states with gun lock requirements had an overall suicide rate of 9.20 per 100,000 (15.28 for those without) and a firearm suicide rate of 2.68 per 100,000 (8.45 for those without), with 28.5% of all suicides resulting from guns (53.4%) for those without. Just as was the case in the first study, we also found significant indirect effects for the laws through the percentage of suicides resulting from guns. This means that the laws might exert their influence on suicide rates by decreasing the frequency with which guns are the method of choice in suicide attempts.

The last thing we did in this paper with respect to firearms and suicide was to examine changes across time in states that implemented or repealed any of the laws. Between 2009 and 2011, four states made relevant law changes: California restricted open carry, DC extended its waiting period, Oklahoma restricted open carry, and South Dakota repealed its waiting period. In all three states that increased their legislation of handguns, the statewide suicide rate decreased in the year immediately following implementation as well as in the total period between implementation and 2013. This was true despite the fact that the national suicide rate increased in each of those years. In contrast, in South Dakota, the repeal of a waiting period law was followed by an immediate 7.6% increase in the statewide suicide rate, which jumped to 8.9% between implementation and 2013. Importantly, this increase was greater than that of the nation as a whole and was in stark contrast to trends within South Dakota in the years leading up to the repeal of the law.

I realize that some of this discussion is heavy on data, and when we think about emotional and difficult to discuss issues, a long list of numbers is often not what we want to see. My rationale for providing so much detail, however, is that without it we are left with emotions and other less objective methods of persuasion. I do not want my points accepted or rejected on the basis of emotions and philosophy. I want to support informed choices based upon a clear understanding of the data. When we take emotion out of the equation and just look at the results, we have an opportunity to learn and move forward.

Before wrapping up this discussion I want to take a moment to describe two more of our studies, but I will do so with less emphasis on statistics. The first is a study that I published this past year with a friend and colleague of mine, Dan Capron. Dan and I wanted to follow up on the work that Joye and I published in one specific way: applying the results to veterans. The bulk of our paper, which was published in 2016 in the *Journal of Psychiatric Research*,[18] was unrelated to gun laws, but one particular analysis tied in nicely. There is already clear evidence that veterans die by suicide at a higher rate than do civilians and that veterans are more likely to use a gun in a suicide attempt. We asked a question that was a natural extension of this: do veterans tend to more heavily saturate the populations of states without specific handgun laws in place? We looked at the same four laws that Joye and I considered and found that, in each case, states without the law in place had populations with a much higher proportion of veterans. Now, we are not arguing that veterans seek out residences in states without gun laws or that the law status of the state influenced whether or not such individuals joined the military. Instead, we noted that soldiers are, on average, more capable of suicide than are civilians and that the tendency of veterans to live in states without specific handgun laws in place might be facilitating their elevated suicide rates by making it easier for them to acquire a gun.

The final study is one that was just recently published in the *American Journal of Public Health*.[19] Along with one of my doctoral students, Sarah Butterworth, Joye and I conducted an additional follow-up to the initial study that we published. In this work, we expanded on the original in two important ways. The first is that we considered change across time, looking at whether law status predicted changes in suicide rates from 2013 (the year of the data from the original study) to 2014 (the most recent year with official suicide data available). The second is that we expanded our list of other variables to consider even further, now controlling for all of the same variables from the original study, as well as gun ownership rates and past year rates of depression and serious suicidal ideation. We found that states with and without gun lock and open carry restriction laws did not differ in their changes in suicide rates from 2013 to 2014. In contrast, states with background check or waiting period laws in place exhibited a significantly different change in their suicide rates between those two years relative to states without those laws. Specifically, whereas states without waiting periods saw an average increase of .71 per 100,000 in their suicide rates from 2013 to 2014, states with waiting periods saw an average decrease of .38 per 100,000. Similarly, whereas states without background checks saw an average increase of .85 per 100,000 from 2013 to 2014, states with background checks saw an average decrease of .29 per 100,000. We also found that the presence of both universal background check and waiting period laws may be more beneficial than the presence of only one or the other. This indicates that there is virtue in having several laws addressing slightly different aspects of the gun acquisition process and that different laws may impact suicide prevention differently. Having universal background checks does not negate the value in having waiting periods and vice versa. Here again, I realize that these seem like small numbers, but when we are considering populations in the millions, they amount to a huge difference in the number of people dying. The results of this study do not indicate that all changes in suicide rates are due to law status, but they point to a potentially vital role for particular forms of legislation relative to others. Specifically, legislation might be most effective when it decreases the odds that individuals will obtain guns (or at least slows down the process). This is reflected in the results for background checks and waiting periods. After a gun has already been acquired, however, it might be that laws are less useful in suicide prevention. At that point, it might be important to utilize nonlegislative methods for reducing risk, which is the focus of the next chapter.

I will conclude this discussion with one final example. In Israel there is compulsory military service for young adults. Several years ago, the Israeli Defense Force (IDF) noted that they were having a problem with young soldiers dying from self-inflicted gunshot wounds when they went home for the weekend. Although not a law change per se, the IDF shifted their policy such that soldiers could no longer bring home their guns on the weekend. Following this shift, the suicide rate among young soldiers dropped by approximately 40%.[20] Soldiers did not simply die using a different method or shoot themselves on a different day of the week. Rather, the IDF identified the pattern, complicated the plausibility of that pattern continuing, and developed a policy shift resulting in far fewer young soldiers dying. The fact that this happened within a military setting is particularly encouraging. This was not a situation in which antigun forces in a low gun ownership area shifted a policy in a moment when firearm suicides were not a pressing problem. Instead, a group of people familiar with firearms simply manipulated behavior in a way that kept people safe.

Taking all of these research findings and combining them into a straightforward understanding of the overall picture can be difficult. In some ways, it might have been easier if I had simply summarized my points in the beginning rather than walking you through so many different publications. But if you already favor gun legislation, you might take my summary at face value without any evidence of its validity, and you then might promote those ideas without any sense of the extent to which they are reasonable. If you are actively opposed to gun legislation, you might have dismissed me out of hand, assuming that I am simply advancing an agenda that runs counter to your beliefs. After all, if I did not give you any actual evidence you could evaluate, why would you simply take my word and change your opinion on an important issue? So my rationale is clear, but that does not make the task easier.

Here is how I would summarize the evidence base for legislative efforts to address the relationship between guns and suicide. Early studies provided fairly strong evidence of an association between laws and suicide rates, but they largely failed to account for other variables that might otherwise explain the results. More recent studies have addressed that limitation quite well, although some of them have found that the presence of a gun wipes out the statistical effects of the presence or absence of specific laws. Some view this as a sign that the laws themselves are irrelevant, but I see these two variables as inseparable in some ways and think it is difficult to see lower gun ownership in states with legislation in place and to simply assume that the law had nothing to do with that ownership rate. Some research has looked at specific laws—the Brady Law for instance—and found mixed evidence for their utility, whereas others have taken a more nuanced approach and considered the variability with which such laws are actually administered across states. Most recently, the research in my lab has highlighted the importance of specific types of laws, noting that those that impact the initial acquisition of a gun might prove the most important.

I have concluded that the research base for legislation is strong and serves as a powerful rationale for exploring these options at the state level (or the federal level if politicians are willing to have that conversation). The evidence is certainly not without flaws—but as you will learn in the next chapter, the same could be said in much stronger terms for the evidence base regarding nonlegislative options. In the United States, guns play an enormous role in suicide, and as I noted in previous chapters, means safety has been perhaps the most important tool in helping address other public health issues such as HIV/ AIDS and lung cancer. It seems obvious that there is a role for means safety in suicide prevention in the United States—be it legislative, non-legislative, or both—and my hope is that decisions regarding how to pursue such efforts will be tied directly to the evidence and not to personal opinions, lobbyists, or political pressures.

Means Safety and Suicide
Prevention Without Legislation

S CIENCE CAN BE A HUMBLING VENTURE. WHEN WE TAKE
our most fervent beliefs, develop them into testable ideas, study
them rigorously, and find that the results come back different than
what we expected, it forces us into a difficult position. Either we
suddenly turn on the science—maybe finding a nitpicky critique of
the study or dismissing the ability of the scientific method to truly
measure an important idea—or we embrace the notion that the world
might not operate the way we thought it did. As a scientist, I have
come to enjoy this aspect of the job. I often tell my doctoral students
that the research results I wrote about in my dissertation were the
complete opposite of what I expected and that not only did this not
cause a problem, it launched a far more interesting line of research
that ultimately paved the way for much of the most exciting work
I have done in my career. As eager young scientists, they are clearly
amenable to this idea and see the fun in chasing truth through challenging our beliefs. When I speak to people who have not decided
to pursue science as their career path, however, I sometimes see a
different response altogether. To many, this process is a threat—a
biased challenge aiming to unjustly alter how the world operates—
and no amount of evidence will sway them.

I have reached a point in my life where I am much more heavily swayed by compelling data than by impassioned arguments, but I realize that this is not always the way of the world. It is clear that research on controversial topics—although well positioned to serve as an unbiased arbiter—is likely to be dismissed by those who disagree with the results. We have seen clear examples of this with climate change, the refuted link between vaccines and autism, evolution, and other topics. Work on guns and suicide undoubtedly fits into this category as well. As I have conducted my research on state gun laws and suicide, I have continuously been aware of the low likelihood that such laws will take hold in my own home. The data simply do not persuade those who firmly maintain a clear vision of the role of guns in our society. Because of this, I often find myself at odds with certain elements of the political culture in Mississippi. At times this is a source of frustration, but at better moments it is motivation to find common ground and search for solutions to big problems that do not involve battling over important but tangentially relevant issues related to guns.

On a personal level, I do not like guns. I would be entirely comfortable with solutions that involve their complete removal from society and would sleep well knowing that my children live in a world in which nobody could use such weapons against them. That simply is not going to happen here, and most relevant to this book, it does not need to happen in order for a place such as Mississippi to embrace gun safety and suicide prevention. Laws are not the only path to gun safety.

In chapter 6, I described a study that Dr. Joye Anestis and I published in the *American Journal of Public Health* in which we showed that state laws involving waiting periods, universal background checks, the use of gun locks, and the restriction of the open carry of handguns are associated with lower overall—again, not just firearm—suicide rates. What I did not mention in that chapter, however, is that we also looked at the relationship between several traffic laws and motor vehicle fatalities. Specifically, we examined whether state laws that ban texting while driving, enforce the use of seatbelts, and ban the use of handheld phones while driving were associated with lower motor vehicle fatalities—and as it turns out, they were not. One way to look at this kind of data is to conclude that those behaviors are simply not related to car accidents and fatalities. Yet there is actually compelling data showing that these behaviors are, in fact, extremely dangerous and that violating the spirit of these laws does increase the likelihood of having a fatal accident. So why then would such laws not be associated with traffic deaths? In my opinion, the answer revolves around a culture of safety that exists with motor vehicles.

When I am driving my car, I wear my seatbelt and strap my children into their car seats, not because I am afraid of getting a ticket but because I want to maximize our odds of remaining safe and healthy should we have an accident. In the same vein, when I am driving, I avoid using my cellphone in unsafe ways not because I fear the legal consequences of violating that principle but because I am afraid that doing otherwise would put myself or others at risk. Yes, the government in some states tells us how we should behave in our cars—privately owned goods, just like personal firearms— but that is not the motivating factor in safe motor vehicle behavior. Individuals in states with and without the specific traffic laws Joye and I examined engage in the safe use of their cars because doing so has become the accepted way to drive, perhaps even reaching the level of moral imperative.

This same culture of safety does not exist with guns, at least not with respect to suicide. This would explain why firearm laws are associated with lower suicide rates, but traffic laws are not associated with motor vehicle deaths. When a culture of safety exists with respect to a certain item or certain group of behaviors, people become intrinsically motivated to behave safely and to encourage similar behavior in others. When that culture of safety does not exist, however, external motivators such as legal consequences become more relevant. In some ways, the lack of a culture of safety around guns is immensely troubling. At times, I struggle to see a path forward in Mississippi on gun safety. At the same time, however, I feel more hopeful when I consider the parallel between the current situation with guns and the relatively recent history of drunk driving.

According to the U.S. Department of Transportation and the National Highway Traffic Safety Administration, more than 25,000 motor vehicle deaths in 1982 were a direct result of drunk driving. Much as is currently the case with firearm suicides relative to overall suicides, drunk driving deaths in the early 1980s represented more than half of all motor vehicle deaths. In fact, in 1982 this figure was almost at 60%. A sizeable part of the problem in the early 1980s and before was a generally permissive viewpoint in American culture toward drunk driving. As someone who largely grew up after this time period, this is difficult for me to imagine, but the nearly universal understanding of the danger and lack of thoughtfulness involved in drunk driving simply was not in place at the time. Indeed, this permissive environment contributed to the founding of Mothers Against Drunk Driving (MADD) shortly after founder Candy Lightner's 13-year-old daughter was killed by a drunk driver in California in 1980.[1] Lightner was appalled by the general acceptance towards drunk driving and the infrequency of severe punishments levied upon even repeat offenders. Shortly after the formation of MADD, California began passing much more restrictive laws regarding drunk driving. By 1999, the total number of alcohol-related traffic fatalities in the United States was less than 15,000, which represented approximately one-third of all accidents.[2]

MADD and similar groups undoubtedly made a positive contribution in advocating for changes in laws and enforcement penalties, but an argument could be made that the precipitous drop in alcohol-related motor vehicle deaths—note that the total went down by more than 40% between 1982 and 1999, despite an ever-increasing national population—was due to a cultural shift in attitudes toward drunk driving. In 1983 the Ad Council launched an advertising campaign that stated, "Drinking and Driving can Kill a Friendship." In the early 1990s the slogan was revised to "Friends Don't Let Friends Drive Drunk."[3] Similarly, in 1989 the Harvard School of Public Health's Center for Health Communication helped develop a national campaign centered on normalizing the idea of designated drivers. In each of these campaigns, efforts were made to promote highly specific behaviors—holding a friend's keys if he's been drinking, securing a ride from an individual who refrains from drinking—geared towards decreasing the number of drunk drivers on the road. These campaigns did not criticize individuals for drinking or demonize alcohol more broadly. There is far from a universal consensus on the societal value of alcohol and any effort to take a stance on that point would have distracted from the common ground: a shared desire to prevent motor vehicle deaths. These were not "alcohol control" or "car control" campaigns, but rather alcohol safety and car safety campaigns centered on safe and responsible use.

It should be noted that around the year 2000, the rate of drunk driving fatalities again began to increase. In response, the Ad Council convened focus groups and determined that the demographic group most responsible for this rise was young adult males who under-estimated the impact of their level of drinking on their ability to drive safely. Having frequently come across answers from partici-pants indicating that they felt safe to drive because they were only "buzzed," the Ad Council developed a new campaign centered on the idea that "Buzzed Driving is Drunk Driving."[4] After peaking at 15,970 alcohol-related motor vehicle fatalities in 2005, the United States saw a decrease to less than 12,000 in 2010, a more than 25% drop in only five years[5] (see Figure 7.1).

There are several aspects of the drunk driving narrative that I think are particularly relevant to the discussion of suicide-related gun safety. As I noted in chapter 4, the overall motor vehicle fatal-ity rate has also declined sharply in recent years. This means that a focus on one specific aspect of motor vehicle deaths—those caused by drunk driving—has had a meaningful impact on the overall occur-rence of deaths in motor vehicles. Other efforts toward improving the safety of vehicles and safe driving by drivers have played important

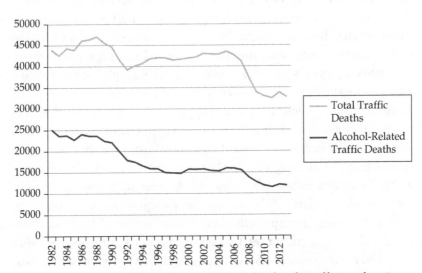

FIGURE 7.1 Total Traffic Fatality and Alcohol-related Traffic Fatality Rates in the United States (1982–2012).

Sources: (1) http://www-fars.nhtsa.dot.gov/Main/reportslinks.aspx
(2) http://www-nrd.nhtsa.dot.gov/Pubs/FARS94.pdf

roles as well, but the focus on alcohol-related deaths represented an important component of a multifaceted effort toward reducing traffic deaths. The parallel with gun suicides is thus quite clear. Much as alcohol-related motor vehicle deaths represented approximately half of all motor vehicle deaths in the early 1980s and focused efforts to address that one aspect of the overall problem yielded impressive results in terms of stemming all motor vehicle deaths, I contend that developing a culture of safety around guns could have a dramatic impact on the overall U.S. suicide rate. Motor vehicle deaths are not simply an alcohol problem, but addressing the prominent role of alcohol illuminated a clear path toward reducing tragedies of individuals dying in their cars. A similar focus on gun safety could, theoretically, produce profound results with respect to the overall national suicide rate.

Safe Storage of Guns Within the Home

Gun-focused means safety measures for suicide could take a number of forms. The simplest involve safe storage. The Means Matter campaign, a program operated through the Harvard University T.H. Chan School of Public Health[6] promotes several specific steps that gun owners can take involving storage. Their first recommendation is that firearms in the home be stored unloaded and locked in a secure location, with ammunition locked in a separate location. A locked cabinet or a gun safe would be good examples of safe storage locations, assuming the integrity of the cabinet or safe was ensured. They also recommend the use of trigger locks—equipment that prevents a person from pulling the trigger of a gun until the mechanism has been unlocked—as an added step in safe storage. In places such as Mississippi—although certainly not exclusively in high gun ownership Southern states—this idea will be met with resistance from some people, particularly those who believe quick access to a firearm is vital to ensure safety in the home from potential threats. There is clear data indicating that this approach is a faulty one and that unlocked guns are more likely to cause the death of a loved one than they are to protect a loved one, or to cause the death (or at least departure) of a home invader. The resistance of people who view guns as vital for home safety, however, likely stems from emotional reasoning, so the simple numbers are unlikely to make much of an impact.

Those looking to encourage safe gun storage by their loved ones (or, in the case of mental health professionals, by therapy clients) might simply look for common ground solutions (e.g., some gun locks require fingerprint recognition, so they can be kept bedside and at least reduce the risk of accidental death by children, even if there is minimal effect on suicide prevention).

The Means Matter campaign argues that safe storage measures could work to reduce firearm suicides due to the speed with which suicidal behavior emerges, but here is a point on which my view diverges from that of the researchers at Means Matter. As I described in chapter 2, scientific evidence quite persuasively dispels the notion that suicidal behavior emerges suddenly, without planning. If it did, safe storage would work because it would slow down a suicidal individual during a sudden and unforeseeable burst of suicidal desire. There is sound logic there, but the data simply do not seem to support that notion (even scientists resist the data sometimes when it goes against long-held beliefs). Instead, I believe safe storage could work simply because it makes a challenging behavior that much harder. Suicide is difficult. Suicidal individuals typically spend an extended period of time working up to the behavior, and many begin an attempt with ambivalent intent. Like any other difficult behavior about which we have mixed feelings, I would argue that simply making suicide more difficult logistically lowers the odds of deciding to move forward. As a parallel, imagine you had to go to an appointment that was stressful and that required driving. Now imagine it starts snowing and the roads—although passable—become a bit more hazardous for driving. Would this make you decide against keeping the difficult appointment, even though it was still feasible to go? Safe storage of a gun does not make it impossible to use a gun in a suicide attempt, but it makes it harder—hopefully just enough to make a difference.

Storing a gun safely—requiring an individual to unlock two safes, load the gun, and release a trigger lock—adds steps and time to a process during which an individual is forced to consider and reconsider his own imminent death and the potential for substantial pain and bodily harm. As Thomas Joiner often told me and my labmates when I was in graduate school, this requires staring down millions of years of evolutionary instincts toward survival without blinking. Extending that staring contest increases the odds that a person will blink because it forces them to muster up more energy to overcome something that many suicidal individuals are not entirely certain they want or are able to do. Indeed, this might be why agitation and other forms of hyperarousal have been found to be imminent risk factors for suicide—characteristics that predict a suicide attempt in the coming hours and moments. Perhaps the surge in energy is needed to enable the individual to follow through with the attempt. Notably, Joiner has also proposed that a drastically reduced blinking rate—not metaphorical blinking as I referenced earlier in this paragraph, but the physical act of blinking—might be a sign of imminent risk for suicide,[7] as such behavior is a sign of intense focus on a thought (in this case, death by suicide) and a "thousand mile stare" with minimal blinking has been observed in individuals in the hours preceding their deaths by suicide[8].

A reasonable response would be to ask whether somebody who truly wants to die would actually be thwarted by a few additional steps. In some cases, I think the answer is "yes," as suicidal intent could feasibly change as a person moves from thinking about suicide to actively attempting to make it happen. People are often surprised how terrifying and difficult suicide attempts are, even when they have been imagining the act for a long time. This phenomenon can be observed in the film *The Bridge*, which shows footage of several individuals—some of whom eventually jumped and others who either changed their minds or were pulled off the edge of the Golden Gate Bridge by good Samaritans—pacing extensively, starting and stopping as they considered whether to follow through on their intentions.

In other cases, however, I would agree that these steps would not prevent the attempt (and likely death). That is why the Means Matter campaign and others—myself included—would argue that gun owners need to weigh the pros and cons of keeping guns in their houses, at least at certain times. I have heard many avid hunters and other gun owners talk about storing their guns outside of the home while they had young children and particularly adolescents as a way to truly diminish their access to lethal means. This still represents a problem for some gun owners though—and is obviously irrelevant to suicidal individuals without children.

Storing Guns Outside the Home in Times of Crisis

Here is where I think the parallel to drunk driving is the closest, and the potential for life saving approaches might be greatest. Another nonlegislative means safety measure involves the voluntary and temporary removal of guns from the home during a crisis period. Much as "Friends don't let Friends Drive Drunk" encouraged a culture of safety around the use of alcohol, a campaign recommending that individuals allow trusted peers to temporarily hold their guns (on their own terms) while they are distressed could help defuse potentially lethal suicidal desire before it results in death. There is compelling evidence that owning a gun does not cause an individual to think about suicide[9,10,11]; however, there is also evidence that gun owners are more than seven times as likely to plan a suicide attempt using a gun than are non-gunowners.[12] In this sense, the risk is not that the gun will cause an individual to become suicidal, but rather than a suicidal individual with a gun is more likely than one without a gun to move to a higher level of risk. Planning is an important step in the transition from suicidal thought to suicide attempt, and the emergence of a detailed plan with a high likelihood of causing death is troubling. Removing a gun from the home during a crisis could therefore interfere with suicide plans during times of elevated distress.

The success of an approach such as this rests upon the establishment of a cultural norm: as much as you trust your friends hold your keys when you have had too much to drink, you trust your friends keep your gun when you are feeling too distressed to safely have it in your home. The process needs to be voluntary, incompatible with the "government is coming to get your guns" narrative—and peers need to be vigilant for cues, much as they are with respect to the sobriety of friends considering getting behind the wheel. The gun is not gone forever and it will be up to the gun owner when to retrieve it, assuming he or she is not still entertaining thoughts of suicide. The process also must not be accusatory. This is not an indictment of a person's self-control or mental strength. It is simply an acknowledgement that when distressed we are more likely to think about suicide, and when those thinking about suicide have ready access to guns, they are substantially more likely to die. As noted in chapter 4, the groups of individuals most at risk for dying by suicide using a gun—men, soldiers, older adults—are less likely to seek out mental health services and more likely to falsely deny suicidal thoughts if they are asked about them. This resistance toward seeking and openly utilizing help undoubtedly stems at least in part from cultural norms regarding what is acceptable to feel, do, and say. If means safety approaches such as this make gun owners feel as though they are being singled out as out of control, mentally unstable, and incapable of taking care of themselves, they will understandably reject the entire process. The fortunate thing is that there is no need to present the situation in such an accusatory way. Temporarily removing one's gun from the home—on one's own terms—is a remarkable demonstration of self-control; this person is taking active steps to solve a potentially deadly problem. The gesture is one of strength, not desperation, and success will hinge upon the extent to which society can present it as such, just like we do with designated drivers.

The Success of Means Safety Hinges upon Credible Publicity

For steps like these to take hold on a societal level, there needs to be substantial buy-in from the gun-owning community itself. Credibility will be low if politicians or non-gun-owning academics such as myself are leading the charge in promoting means safety. My experience in Mississippi speaks directly to this point. On several occasions I have attempted to initiate conversations with individuals in the gun-owning community about increasing education efforts on guns and suicide. I have approached individuals involved in concealed carry and hunting license education classes, where gun owners are routinely provided with information on gun safety as it relates to accident prevention. My style of speaking is that of someone from the Northeast, and because of this, within seconds of beginning a conversation it often becomes apparent to the person I am speaking with that I am not local. I am immediately established as an outsider, and on top of that, I want to talk about two profoundly sensitive topics: guns and suicide. On one occasion, I called a local Mississippi woman advertising gun safety training services, and she quickly left the conversation before I could finish two sentences. I was only able to start it back up after e-mailing her links to editorials I have written advocating for gun safety (e.g., safe storage) rather than the banning of guns. Sensitivity is so high on the issue of guns that many immediately assume that I am about to begin a battle over the Second Amendment, and my identity as a nonlocal, non-gun-owning academic does little to help matters.

A consequence of the difficulties in starting such conversations is that we lose sight of the common ground we share and of the many past successes from which we could all learn. For instance, in the state of Mississippi efforts at eliminating accidental gun deaths have been remarkably successful. The Mississippi Department of Wildlife, Fisheries, and Parks offers free hunter education classes at locations across the state.[13] Such classes involve extensive training in how to properly use and handle a gun. The educators and gun owners take the safe handling of firearms seriously and this cultural value toward the avoidance of accidents has produced positive results. From 2011 through 2014, there were a total of 75 accidental firearm deaths in Mississippi, an average of less than 19 each year. Each of those 75 deaths is tragic, but that number is astoundingly small compared to firearm suicides over the same period and a true testament to the efforts of this state agency and others toward encouraging individuals to take the necessary steps to avoid firearm accidents.

The same success has not been apparent with suicide. The free classes offered throughout Mississippi on gun safety—to my knowledge—do not involve information on suicide prevention. Indeed, several educators have explicitly told me that suicide prevention is outside of their goals, as suicide is seen as unrelated to gun safety. Many gun owners I have spoken to are unaware of the association between guns and suicide, and yet during the same 2011–2014 timeframe discussed above with respect to accidental firearm deaths, there were a total of 1,094 suicide deaths by firearms in Mississippi, an average of nearly 275 each year (see Figure 7.2). In fact, in 2013 a higher percentage of statewide suicides resulted from gunshot wounds in Mississippi (72%) than in any other state in the nation.[14] How many of those deaths could have been prevented if gun safety courses included a suicide prevention component?

I will point out, however, that not all of my interactions with gun owners have been unsuccessful. Indeed, in 2016 an official from the Mississippi Department of Wildlife, Fisheries, and Parks—the same person who oversees the accident prevention and gun safety education

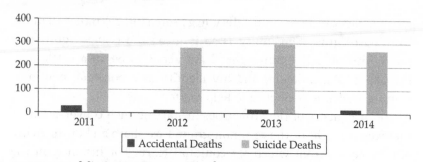

FIGURE 7.2 Mississippi Firearm Deaths, 2011–2014.

Source: https://webappa.cdc.gov/sasweb/ncipc/DataRestriction_inj.html

courses offered statewide—visited my lab and gave a tremendous presentation on the mechanics of firearms. He was also highly supportive of our efforts. Furthermore, the Department of Defense has demonstrated a remarkable openness to work that addresses the role of firearms in soldiers' deaths, and I have had the pleasure of speaking with officials from the DoD in several forums regarding potential policy changes and ways to assess the efficacy of such approaches. Talking about guns and suicide is tricky when we do not share the same views, but once everyone makes it clear that we respect one another's right to an opinion, the defenses can fall away fairly quickly.

I would argue that the disconnect between firearm accident prevention and firearm suicide prevention seems to be driven at least in part by a lack of buy-in from the gun-owning community on suicide means safety practices. The numbers in the table above show us that when gun owners voluntarily work to develop safety standards, they are impressively effective at implementing them on a broad scale and preventing deaths. But so far we have not seen similar efforts toward suicide prevention. The mission then must be getting academic research results into the hands of influential gun rights advocates and motivating large-scale efforts to use that information to support suicide prevention work. Remember my point from the beginning of this chapter: even the most compelling data from the most rigorous studies can fall flat in discussions on emotionally charged issues.

We need not be without hope that means safety efforts in Mississippi and other states may yet take hold, as success has already been seen with related measures in other parts of the country. A particularly promising example comes from New Hampshire. In 2009 three people died by suicide in a single week using guns purchased from the same store just hours before their deaths. The owner of the store was understandably horrified, and he and others, including members of the Means Matter campaign mentioned earlier in this chapter, came together to develop a plan to prevent similar outcomes in the future.[15] Sponsored by the New Hampshire Gun Firearm Safety Coalition, the project—often referred to as the Gun Shop Project—aims to educate gun shop owners on the warning signs of suicide, enabling them to make informed decisions about whether an individual may be in crisis. The project also encourages gun shop owners to display suicide prevention materials.

The effectiveness of campaigns such as this remains untested, a clear rationale for increased funding into studies on gun violence and its prevention, but early results are promising. The New Hampshire coalition sent suicide prevention materials to shops across the state. Six months later, coalition members made unannounced visits to each shop and found that 48% of them had at least one piece of educational material displayed inside the store: this was a remarkable level of participation given that the materials cover an emotionally charged topic and were provided to shop owners unsolicited. From there, the coalition investigated the factors that influenced the willingness of gun shop owners to display these materials and found that owners who believed that temporarily removing access to firearms would be useful in preventing suicide were more likely than those without such beliefs to display the materials (69% vs. 41%[16]). This tells us two things. First, educating gun shop owners and others involved in the selling of and training in firearms on the relationship between guns and suicide may increase the likelihood that the gun owning community itself will voluntarily take an active and leading role in means safety efforts. Second, given that 41% of gun shop owners who did not believe temporary removal of guns would be helpful at reducing suicides *still* displayed suicide prevention materials in their stores, there is reason to believe that people do not need to fundamentally alter their beliefs in order to decide to participate in suicide prevention efforts.

The Path Forward

In early 2016 I was invited to give a keynote address at an event at Washington University in St. Louis as part of that institution's

year-long Gun Safety Initiative. In response to the death by homicide of a former student, the university decided to bring in academic
experts and invested parties from the community to discuss gun
violence—including suicide—and to develop strategies for how to
effect change. The university saw its role as bringing together differing perspectives from different professions and to draw upon that
diversity to develop tangible plans. The event was remarkably inspiring. At a workgroup dinner, fellow members of the panel discussed
potential roles for law enforcement, physicians, veterans groups, and
a broad array of others who come into contact with gun owners on
a regular basis. For law enforcement, we discussed the potential for
creating safe drop locations in police departments for suicidal individuals to legally, safely, and temporarily leave their personal firearms when they are in crisis and need to remove the gun(s) from
their home. Although not discussed at this event, I cannot help but
wonder whether having similar drop boxes in gun shops might prove
even more influential (if implemented safely), as it might lower concerns among suicidal gun owners that they would lose their guns or
be subjected to legal consequences or unwanted psychological assessments and treatments. With physicians, we discussed the need for
regular and culturally sensitive means safety counseling with those
experiencing suicidal thoughts in order to decrease their ability to
transition to suicidal behaviors. With veteran groups, we discussed
the notion of developing relationships similar to "battle buddies,"
in which veterans check in with one another and agree to discuss
removing weapons from the home during times of distress.

There are many more groups of people who could play important
roles in developing a widespread culture of safety around guns and
suicide, with an emphasis on means safety practices (See Table 7.1).
If the conversation becomes one of gun control rather than suicide
prevention, it is almost certain to fail, but if it is one that becomes
"gun safety for gun owners," a campaign led at least in part by prominent gun owners to emphasize safe and responsible ownership, an
opportunity exists for a meaningful and sustained reduction in the
national suicide rate.

Because there are so many stakeholders and potential points of
contact for means safety interventions, it is vital to communicate to
gun owners a single, simple message, either at a national level or
as a series of statewide initiatives specific to particular regions: you

TABLE 7.1 Stakeholders and Their Possible Roles in Means Safety Efforts

Group	Potential Role in Means Safety Efforts
Ad Council and Similar Groups	Normalizing and publicizing the notion of gun-focused means safety
Gun Rights Advocates (e.g., NRA)	Leadership roles in promoting means safety for suicide prevention Increasing credibility of the message Framing means safety as healthy problem solving and sign of strength
Educators	Increasing national knowledge on suicide risk factors
Family/Peers	Vigilance for distress in gun owner—willingness to initiate means safety
Health-care Providers	Inquiring about access to means with distress patients Engaging in means safety counseling
Legislators	Ensuring state laws provide for legal locations for temporary and voluntary storage of personal firearms during times of distress
Media	Increasing the role of suicide in gun violence discussions Highlighting the research supporting means safety

need not give up your rights in order to help reduce firearm suicides. Means safety must represent a cultural shift akin to what we saw nationally starting in the early 1980s relating to drunk driving. Independent of Second Amendment debates, a national priority must be safe, responsible gun ownership among those who decide to own guns and, as a corollary, vigilance on the part of family and friends of gun owners for signs of distress (and perhaps education on risk factors for suicide). An Ad Council campaign about gun-centered means safety approaches to suicide prevention could be the catalyst for a larger, national conversation. Leadership roles by prominent gun rights advocates—perhaps even the NRA itself—would lend credibility to the conversation and ease fears that such efforts are thinly veiled attempts to "get the guns." A concerted effort to frame voluntary means safety efforts by distressed gun owners as a show of strength—proactive healthy problem solving and a sign of responsible gun ownership—could increase the willingness of those in need to take steps to diminish their own risk of suicide. A decreased fear of openly discussing suicide could inspire health-care providers to ask distressed patients about access to lethal means and engage in means safety counseling when appropriate.

I cannot say with any certainty what the odds are that a multifaceted means safety effort like the one I outlined above will take hold in the coming years. I also cannot promise that such an effort would definitively reduce the national suicide rate. That being said, given successes with similar approaches to other problems, and the fact that we are now more than a decade into a streak of annual increases in our national suicide rate, a concerted effort to translate this vision into reality and examine its utility in suicide prevention seems like a potentially high- value effort that involves no apparent risk. No coherent argument against this approach has ever been articulated to me, so the primary obstacles appear to revolve around a general lack of knowledge about the scope and nature of the role of guns in suicide. Suicide prevention has to become a national priority before suicide prevention efforts such as this will take hold.

Disarming Common Concerns
About Means Safety

F ROM AN EARLY AGE, MY SON HAS CONSIDERED HIMSELF
a scientist. When he uses that term, he does not envision my
job or anything related to what I do, so it is not simply a matter
of parroting his parents. He sees this more as a matter of invent-
ing potions that accomplish important tasks or harnessing DNA to
bring dinosaurs back from extinction. Nevertheless, he places great
value in studying topics to understand them and develop solutions
to anything problematic or incomplete. Starting in kindergarten, we
enrolled him in a private Catholic school because the location and
quality of education were the best available fit. The trick here is that
religion is infused into the educational experiences at his school,
and since the age of three, my son has also firmly and consistently
declared himself an atheist. I respect that he has come to an early
conclusion on this. We have always told him to believe what he wants
to believe and have presented material from a range of perspectives.
And he has always been unwavering in his stance. My son and I have
regularly had conversations about respecting the opinions of others
and acknowledging their right to have a perspective that differs from
ours, as long as their perspective is not hurting anyone.

I feel good about these interactions and believe that they have taught him an important lesson about tolerance and stepping outside of his comfort zone. At the same time, I also have a fear that sits in the back of my head each time we talk about this. My son is still probably a bit too young to fully grasp the nuance of this point, but the bottom line is that not all opinions are equally "correct," and even when they are not harming anyone, not all ideas deserve equal weight. This point is reflected in the daily experience of many Americans as they sift through social media feeds and news stories. The concepts of "fake news" and "alternative facts" have—at least in my experience—become constant considerations in many conversations and in many of the stories I read. A willingness of some to accept stories of questionable veracity (or worse yet, being promoted despite substantial contradictions or falsehoods) and a constant barrage of unreasonable accusations of lying levied toward accurate news reports has created an atmosphere in which many either do not know what to believe or base their opinions of stories on the extent to which these stories align with their views. Evidence is an afterthought. This environment has, to some extent, been a source of tension for those of us who want to be open minded to others' ideas but who also place an emphasis on the role of evidence in determining opinions. In the end, some ideas are wrong and need to be dismissed, even if that is uncomfortable. When a cherished belief is demonstrated to be incorrect, this is not simply a sign that the storyteller is unleashing "fake news."

When it comes to guns and suicide, not all views are equal, and some opinions that are not borne out of any ill will toward others are nonetheless unsound. I say this not simply because I disagree with these perspectives or find them difficult to reconcile with my own beliefs. I say this because scientists have heard those perspectives, tested them, and repeatedly refuted them. The important thing to keep in mind is that I am not arguing that it is unreasonable to hold certain opinions prior to having access to accurate information. All of us have felt certain about specific ideas, only to be confronted with the possibility that we were wrong. My point is that once we are presented with unambiguous evidence that we are incorrect, it is time to move on, and defiantly maintaining a stance in the face of all evidence is simply not a reasonable approach to life and death matters such as suicide. I want to devote this final chapter to dispelling some of the most commonly believed myths about guns and suicide. If you currently hold some of these opinions, you may find my use of the term "myth" frustrating, but I am hopeful that the evidence I provide to support my contentions will be persuasive.

Means Substitution

By far the most common argument against means safety is what scientists refer to as "means substitution"—if somebody really wants to die by suicide and we take away his preferred method (such as guns), he will simply find another way to do it. Though incorrect, this view does seem intuitive, reasonable. This line of thinking generally embraces suicide as a frantic, impulsive act and underestimates the degree of planning and resolve required to overcome perhaps our most powerful genetic imperative—surviving and maintaining the physical integrity of our bodies.

Understand that I make no claim that suicide is somehow admirable when I write that it requires resolve—I am simply acknowledging a reality of the behavior. If suicide were easy, far more people would die by suicide; thousands upon thousands of people in the United States every day experience a relentless and overwhelming desire to die but for any number of reasons will never make a suicide attempt. The relative few who are able to translate their suicidal thoughts into suicidal behavior tend to have a specific vision for their attempt. An argument could be made that this is less true for individuals who make less lethal attempts—remember that the less planned an attempt is the less lethal it tends to be. Additionally, as my own research has shown, individuals who indicate that they definitely wanted to die during their most recent non-lethal suicide attempt typically first started thinking about making a suicide attempt using the method they actually ended up using nearly a year before that attempt. The plan had been building—perhaps off and on—for an extended period of time before it resulted in actual behavior.

Plans for suicide—visions of how it will be done—afford individuals an opportunity to become less daunted by the act. Means safety efforts, which make commonly used and highly lethal methods for suicide less lethal or more difficult to access during a suicide attempt, interrupt that planning process; in doing so, these efforts render a daunting behavior that much more difficult. Like anything else in life, when we feel ambivalence toward a possible future behavior and something in our environment makes that behavior more difficult, the odds that we will engage in the behavior go down. For instance, if I come across an amusing meme online while sitting at my computer in my house, my first inclination is often to show my wife in hopes of making her chuckle. If, however, I discover that she is upstairs, it is entirely possible (pathetic though this may be) that I will opt to remain where I am rather than seeking her out. Chances are the meme was not particularly life altering and I will forget about it moments later, thereby preventing me from ever making the effort to share this aspect of the Internet with my wife. In this case, my emotions surrounding the subject were not particularly strong, and the subject was obviously not particularly important; however, the point remains that making the desired option harder made me opt against doing it. This does not mean that I will never encounter the meme in the future and make another effort, but it does mean that a simple obstacle can at times prevent a behavior. This same principle applies when the stakes are much higher and our emotions much stronger—when somebody prefers suicide to life but suicide becomes harder than anticipated (or at least harder than a person can manage), he or she becomes increasingly less likely to engage in a suicide attempt.

Perhaps because suicide is so difficult and daunting, suicidal individuals tend to develop a preference for a specific method for suicide and, in some cases, even a particular place (a specific bridge, for example)[1]. Disrupting peoples' ability to utilize their preferred method for suicide largely changes the meaning and feasibility of the behavior. This is borne out by the fact that when people make more than one suicide attempt in their lifetimes, they are likely to repeatedly utilize the same method rather than build up to a more lethal approach.[2] Earlier in the book I noted that individuals who die by suicide using a gun are less likely than those who die using other methods to have had a previous suicide attempt. This is because guns are highly lethal but also because individuals who survived previous attempts using other methods do not typically transition to guns in subsequent attempts. The method itself matters and interfering with its use before an attempt can ultimately save a life.

One of the most cited scientific articles on this topic was published in 2005 by Mark Daigle in the journal *Accident Analysis and Prevention.*[3] Daigle reported that suicide rates went down in the United States and in Japan following the detoxification of natural gas—just as they had in the United Kingdom.[4,5] In each country there was no evidence that those hindered in their efforts to die by natural gas poisoning instead opted to use other methods. Daigle also noted that restrictions in the sale of certain drugs—typically by making those that would be lethal in overdose available only by prescription—has resulted in reductions in suicide by drug overdose, with no discernable increase in deaths by other suicide methods. These effects were also noted in Australia,[6] Japan,[7] and the United Kingdom.[8]

With respect to guns in particular, recall the findings I discussed in the previous two chapters. When the Israeli Defense Force instituted a policy prohibiting soldiers from bringing their firearms home with them on the weekend, they saw a 40% decrease in their suicide rate among the most vulnerable population (young soldiers), with no subsequent increases in other methods or even on other days. In the studies that I published looking at specific state laws regulating handgun ownership and statewide suicide rates, the overall suicide rates were lower in states with laws in place—not just the firearms suicide rates. If individuals were simply choosing another method when guns were less available, the firearms suicide rate would go down, but the overall rate would remain stagnant, as those deaths would be displaced rather than eliminated.

A reasonable concern in response to my previous point is that it is not entirely clear that all means safety efforts have an effect on the overall suicide rate. Would this then be evidence of means substitution? No. The extent to which a means safety effort impacts the overall suicide rate is going to depend heavily upon the commonality of the method. An extremely effective bridge barrier for instance, which eliminates lethal jumps from a popular suicide site and results in no increases in suicides at other locations or by other means, will have little to no effect on the national overall suicide rate because jumps from high places account for such a small percentage of U.S. suicides (although there may be changes in the rate in that specific location—a highly volatile number because so few suicides take place in a given spot in a given year). This does not change the life-saving nature of the intervention or imply that individuals simply died by other means. Instead, it highlights the importance of committing first to means safety efforts focused on the most common causes of death by suicide. By no means am I unsupportive of efforts that focus on less common methods, but means safety measures in the United States focused on anything other than guns will quite simply result in fewer lives saved. We will be working to prevent far rarer events and missing a large proportion of suicide deaths.

Unconvinced? Or know someone who might be? For the sake of argument, let's assume that you remain skeptical about the effectiveness of means safety. There is still a justifiable argument in favor of large scale gun-focused means safety efforts within the United States as a primary suicide prevention approach. Given the lethality of firearms, the reality is that even if means substitution was common, means safety efforts targeting guns would nevertheless result in an enormous savings in lives. No other suicide method is as deadly, so even if every single person who would have otherwise used a gun found a different suicide method, many would survive by virtue of the lower lethality of their backup method. Given that 90% of those who survive an attempt never make another one, this means that a huge number of lives would likely be saved. Means safety does not change the way people die by suicide—it prevents their deaths by suicide.

What About Asia?

Another common form of resistance to firearms-focused means safety rests on the nature of suicide in several Asian countries, including Japan and South Korea. Gun laws in these two countries are quite strict and gun ownership is low, but their suicide rates far exceed that of the United States.

As Figure 8.1 illustrates, Japan's suicide rate far exceeded that of the United States from 1985 to 2009. The story is different with South Korea's rate, which was far below that of the United States in 1985 but surpassed the U.S. rate beginning in the late 1990s; South Korea now has a suicide rate more than double that of the United States. This is a rather stunning set of statistics representing a particularly horrifying upward trend in South Korea. In a study published in *BMC Public Health*[9] in 2009, Jin-Won Kwon, Heeran Chun, and Sung-il Cho noted that, from 1986–2005, the South Korean suicide

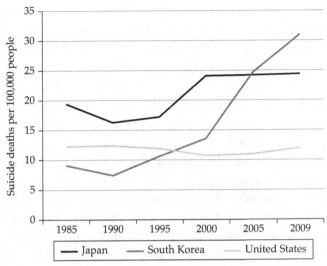

FIGURE 8.1 Suicide Rates in Japan, South Korea, and the United States.

Sources: (1) Kwon, J., Chun, H., & Cho, S. (2009). A closer look at the increase in suicide rates in South Korea from 1986-2005. *BMC Public Health*, 9, 72
(2) https://www.cdc.gov/injury/wisqars/fatal.html
(3) https://data.oecd.org/healthstat/suicide-rates.htm

rate increased by 98% (15.3 per 100,000 to 30.3 per 100,000) for men and 124% (5.8 per 100,000 to 13.0 per 100,000) for women.

There are equally pronounced differences between these countries in terms of gun ownership and gun legislation. In Japan, for instance, gun ownership is nearly nonexistent. As detailed by Max Fisher in an article in *The Atlantic* in 2012,[10] the process for acquiring and keeping a gun in Japan is remarkably intense, involving attendance at a day-long class, passing a written exam and a shooting range test, passing a mental fitness test and a drug test in a hospital setting, and undergoing an extensive background check. If these hurdles are cleared, applicants are then able to buy a shotgun or an air rifle. All other forms of firearms (handguns, assault rifles) are explicitly banned in the country. Furthermore, any gun bought has to be registered with police, the location of the gun and ammunition must be documented, and the gun and ammunition must be stored separately and in locked locations. Police then inspect the gun annually and the gun owner must retake the class and exams every three years. Gun ownership is so low that even gangs in Japan tend to eschew the use of guns. By any measure this is a high level of regulation, and it has produced its desired effect; as Fisher noted in his article, gun deaths are so low in Japan that only two firearm-related deaths were reported in the entire country in 2006. Gun ownership and gun suicides are essentially nonexistent in Japan, and yet its national suicide rate, 17.3 per 100,000 in 2016,[11] has remained quite high for decades (it should be noted, however, that this rate has steadily decreased in recent years).

The situation is not much different in South Korea. There, citizens can only buy hunting guns and air rifles, much like in Japan, and those weapons can only be stored at home during hunting season. For the remainder of the year, guns must be stored at the police station. The penalty for illegally possessing a firearm in South Korea involves multiple years of jail time. GunPolicy.org collects data on gun ownership[12] on a country-by-country basis, and their numbers highlight the extent to which gun ownership and acquisition restrictions have limited access to guns in Japan and South Korea relative to the United States. In South Korea there are an estimated 1.1 privately owned firearms (legal and illegal) for every 100 people, which translates to a total of approximately 510,000 (a total of approximately 300,000 guns are legally registered, with 0.62 legally owned guns for every 100 people). Of those 510,000 guns, only 1,758 were registered handguns. This makes South Korea 149th out of 178 countries ranked in terms of gun ownership. In Japan, the same survey estimates that there are 710,000 privately owned guns (legal and illegal), which translates to 0.6 guns per 100 people. Astoundingly, only 77 handguns are reported to be in the possession of Japanese civilians. Overall, GunPolicy.org places Japan at 164th out of 178 countries in terms of gun ownership.

The numbers in the United States are quite different. As I mentioned earlier, there are an estimated 270 million to 310 million privately owned firearms in the United States, approximately 114 million of which are handguns. This translates to 101.05 firearms per 100 people, meaning there are more guns than people in the United States. Given these numbers, it is no surprise that the United States was ranked first out of 178 countries in terms of gun ownership.

These figures may reasonably be a cause for concern for those suspicious of whether gun-focused means safety—and particularly legislation—represents a viable tool in suicide prevention in the

United States. After all, if countries that have essentially abolished private gun ownership have higher suicide rates than the United States, how could guns be the key to reducing the U.S. national suicide rate?

I will go into more detail on Japan and South Korea shortly. First, however, I propose that guns and suicide relate differently to one another in the United States versus Japan and South Korea and that this can be explained by cultural differences and the degree to which guns represent an important part of national cultural identities. I am not arguing that the natural state of suicidal thinking involves guns and that making guns less accessible renders suicide impossible because humans could not possibly devise other ways to cause their own deaths. Suicide occurred long before guns were invented and would continue to occur if they were completely eliminated. My point is that suicide would occur far less often in a specific place—the United States—if gun ownership there were curtailed or, if nothing else, if gun owners in the United States stored their guns more safely and removed them from the home during times of crisis. I believe that guns are so widespread and accessible, and also that Americans are so much more comfortable with the notion of guns than people in the rest of the world, that guns have become much more entwined with the ideas of death and suicide for Americans than they have in other locations. As David Klonsky notes, access to and comfort with lethal means can facilitate the transition from thinking about suicide to engaging in a suicide attempt, and nowhere else in the world are people more comfortable with and exposed to guns than in the United States. The cultures in general and gun culture in particular in Japan and South Korea—both non-Western countries—are vastly different than what we experience in the United States; given this, it should not be surprising that their vision of and path to death might differ as well.

What about nations that are culturally similar to the United States? I have already discussed the means safety efforts of the IDF in Israel, but another worthwhile comparison is Australia. Now, just because it aligns with my point about guns and suicide does not make this nation the best example. That would be cherry picking evidence, and I have no interest in doing that. I chose Australia here for two reasons. First, we have a chance to look at the effect over time of a fairly recently implemented large-scale change in gun policies and gun ownership. Second, Australia—although quite different in many ways—is much more similar culturally to the United States than are Japan and South Korea. In this sense, vulnerabilities to suicide and the phenomenology of suicide can reasonably be expected to map on more closely to what we see in the United States.

In 1996 Australia implemented the National Firearms Agreement, which heavily restricted automatic and semiautomatic weapons and implemented firearm registration and licensure requirements. Furthermore, the government initiated a massive buyback program that allowed Australian citizens to sell their guns back to the government without penalty. In the years following the buyback effort, Australia's firearm suicide rate dropped by 74%, but some researchers have noted that the suicide rate was already falling prior to the implementation of that program (see Figure 8.2). This is true: the firearm suicide rate was 3.0 per 100,000 in 1991 and had dropped to 2.1 per 100,000 in 1996. Equally true, however, is that the rate decrease accelerated dramatically after the buyback.[13,14] From 1996 to 1998, the rate dropped to 1.3 per 100,000 and, in 2014 that number was down to 0.7 per 100,000. The 30% drop from 1991 to 1996 should not be overlooked, but it is clearly less notable than the 67% decrease from 1996 to 2014 (the rate actually first reached 0.7 in 2005 too, so

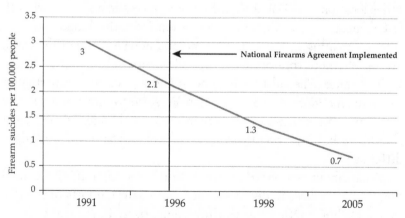

FIGURE 8.2 Australian Firearms Suicide Rate (1991–2005).

Sources: (1) Chapman, S., Alpers, P., Agho, K., & Jones, M. (2006). Australia's 1996 gun law reforms: Faster falls in firearm deaths, firearm suicides, and a decade without mass shootings. *Injury Prevention, 12,* 365–372.
(2) Leigh, A., & Neill, C. (2010). Do gun buybacks save lives? Evidence from panel data. *American Law and Economics Review.* doi: 10.1093/aler/ahq013

the drop occurred quite quickly and has since been sustained for a decade).

Another important point is that registration of handguns was already required prior to the National Firearms Agreement, and handguns are responsible for the majority of firearm suicides. In other words, the National Firearms Agreement was followed by massive reductions in firearm suicides even though the type of guns most often used for suicide—handguns—were already required to be registered. I should also note that the overall suicide rate, which peaked at 14.6 per 100,000 in 1997 stood at 12.2 per 100,000 in 2014.[15] That is only a 16.4% decrease in suicides overall, which indicates that some means substitution might be occurring here, but again not enough to offset the number of lives saved. In 2013, however, the suicide rate was 10.9 per 100,000, meaning that before this most recent increase (to the highest rate in 13 years[16]), the overall suicide rate had dropped by over 25%. Indeed, if you look at the data from across the early 21st century in Australia, it is evident that the overall suicide rate has hovered around 10 per 100,000 each year, in direct contrast to the annual increases seen in the United States.[17] Simply put, the National Firearms Agreement in Australia was followed by a sustained drop not only in firearm suicides but also in overall suicides.

Going back to the GunPolicy.org numbers, from 1996 to 1997 (the year the gun laws changed), the number of privately owned firearms in Australia decreased from 3.2 million to 2.5 million, a 22% drop in a single year. Similarly, the rate of gun ownership dropped from 17.58 per 100 to 13.58 per 100 that year. These numbers creeped back up to 3.1 million guns and a gun ownership rate of 15 per 100 by 2005, but there was a pronounced and immediate decrease in gun ownership after the initiation of the National Firearms Act. Even with that large drop, however, guns remained substantially more common in Australia than in Japan or South Korea; Australia was ranked 42nd of 178 countries for its number of privately owned firearms.

Before returning to Japan and South Korea, it is worth noting something important about the successes in Australia. The National Firearms Agreement was not a suicide prevention effort. It was a direct response to a mass shooting, and much like the situation in the United States, efforts to control gun deaths in Australia were largely framed as an effort to reduce homicide. Despite the regrettable tendency for politicians and policymakers to overlook suicide when discussing guns, gun safety measures that do not even target suicide appear to have profound effects on suicide rates. The method matters. Imagine what we might be able to accomplish through efforts that actually focus on suicide prevention.

Going back to Japan and South Korea, it is important to go beyond simply noting that our cultures, particularly surrounding guns, are different, and leave it at that. So why are these Asian countries' suicide rates so high despite such low levels of gun ownership? First, consider Japan's, cultural history of suicide. For centuries, the notion of honorably taking one's own life, or *seppuku*, was a near-sacred ritual in Japanese culture. Initially specific to Samurai, *seppuku* is the act of intentionally disemboweling oneself by inserting a sharp blade into the abdomen and slicing it open from one side to the other. Sometimes the ritual involved spectators. The individual was expected to experience the pain quietly as he bled to death. *Seppuku* was typically used in an effort to avoid capture and likely torture by enemies, but it was also seen as an appropriate response to criminal offenses and shame. Speaking to Japan's present-day suicide rates, as recently as the early 20th century, prominent members of the Japanese military engaged in *seppuku*, and the practice is also not entirely unrelated to a more recent phenomenon: kamikaze attacks. As the conflict in the Pacific was reaching its conclusion during the Second World War, and the Allied forces were approaching Japan with superior equipment and much greater numbers, Japanese soldiers began using themselves as weapons to inflict greater damage on the enemy than they could with ammunition alone. The most famous form of kamikaze attack was that of pilots intentionally crashing their planes into warships, resulting in the death of the pilot but more importantly inflicting substantial damage to the Allied forces and possibly mass casualties. Here we see a Japanese tradition, especially prominent in the military, of intentionally approaching death when the circumstances, as evaluated according to a specific set of cultural values and norms, demanded.

If you think back to chapter 2, you might recall my discussion of Thomas Joiner's interpersonal theory of suicide and the notion of perceived burdensomeness. Joiner argued that suicidal individuals tend to make a decision that their deaths would be more valuable than their continued lives. In Western culture, at least with respect to the typical suicide death, that line of thinking is fairly abstract.

In the case of *seppuku* and kamikaze deaths, however, the calculation appears quite clear, driven by combat scenarios or specific violations of an honor code. Given the collectivist nature of Japanese culture, in which people tend to view themselves as part of the group as much if not more than they think of themselves as individuals, the rationale for this becomes clearer. A person sees his or her death as benefitting the group and so opts to die. This behavior is actually mirrored in nature in the behavior of other animals that when injured or ill (or when the group is threatened) intentionally place themselves in dangerous or deadly situations to increase the odds of group survival. Joiner noted that members of eusocial species—a term defined differently by different sources but largely meaning species in which individuals take on specific roles and work towards the preservation of the group—will go so far as to deliberately and fatally wound themselves to save the group (for instance stinging insects that die upon attacking an invasive predator). Others will minimize food consumption and remove themselves from the group when sick to reduce exposure to pathogens and to preserve resources for those better able to survive (certain species of ants have been known to do this). Some will attack larger animals certain to kill them when the defenses of the larger group are compromised, and such an approach could provide a possible escape for others. Naked mole rats, for instance, will attack snakes and other predators during moments when burrows are exposed and incomplete, thereby leaving the entire colony vulnerable.[18]

Although not perfectly analogous with suicide, these behaviors are not unrelated. In some species, causing one's own death to benefit the group is a natural instinct. In the same way, in some cultures, the notion of ending one's own life seems to be less foreign, and an argument could be made that although collectivism encourages identifying with others (remember the importance of social connections to our well-being), the reduced focus on the importance of the individual might also facilitate action in response to an individual's sense that his or her death might benefit others. Viewed through this lens, suicide—one form of self-inflicted death—would not necessarily be considered a problematic behavior. Indeed, even the predominant religions within Japan lack any overtly negative views of suicide, with both Shinto[19] and Buddhist[20] doctrines appearing largely ambivalent toward it (and potentially maintaining positive views towards suicide as an act of self-sacrifice for the good of others). This stands in stark contrast to Christian doctrines that describe suicide as a sin worthy of damnation. It should be noted, however, that the protective effects of Christian religious identification have been shown to be due to attendance in church services (a social connection) rather than beliefs in the immorality of the behavior. In this sense, religions that condone (even passively) suicide may lead a suicidal individual to feel that suicide has value and this accepting view may prove more powerful than any potential protective effect of a religion describing suicide as immoral.

Fast forward to modern life in Japan, and these trends can be seen clearly. In recent years the phenomenon of *hikikomori* has garnered increasing attention in Japan. *Hikikomori* involves severe social withdrawal and a lack of communication with others in the absence of mental illness. I have a difficult time understanding it, but that likely stems from the fundamentally different cultural lens through which I view the world. Indeed, researchers have reported evidence that *hikikomori* is what is known as a "culturally bound" syndrome that does not have a correlating mental illness in the Western classification system.[21]

In a collectivist culture in which individuals' withdrawal from the group can be seen as noble and for the greater good, and in which there exists a strong emphasis on taking responsibility for one's own flaws and bad acts (as well as relatively low levels of disapproval of suicide from a religious perspective), suicide risk becomes a larger concern. Combine this with a general cultural trend toward internalizing distress, and the circumstances are in place for suicidal desire to flourish in Japan. Add the economic struggles of Japan over the past two decades, and suicide risk further increases, with the elderly particularly likely to conclude that suicide represents the clearest path toward contributing to their families. Japanese life insurance companies are permissive compared with those in the United States in paying out in response to suicide deaths; incentives in place in some ways actually favor suicide for adults in financial peril.[22] (I do not believe that changes to U.S. insurance practices to emulate the Japanese model would increase suicidal behavior in the United States, though I am not in favor of withholding life insurance payments when a person dies by suicide.)

With a cultural framework differing substantially from that of the United States, South Korea has also experienced several shifts that appear to have had a substantial impact on its national suicide rate. As noted by Kwon and colleagues in an article I referred to earlier in this chapter, a potentially dangerous trend in Korean culture involving the care of the elderly maps quite well onto increases in its suicide rate. In addition to South Korea's severe financial crisis in 1997, the nation has seen the steady erosion of a prominent cultural concept, known as *Hyo*. Confucian in origin, *Hyo* is the idea of respect for the elderly and the sense of responsibility for their care. Historically this has been demonstrated by a willingness of adults to care for their parents in old age. The nation's loss of *Hyo* has occurred alongside the development and implementation of a system of care intended to assist older adults, the Law of Elderly Welfare, that has proven insufficient in terms of its stated goals (e.g., home care, pensions). As a result, adults above the age of 65 represent a disproportionate segment of the workforce in South Korea, with retirees forced into jobs with low quality of postretirement life in order to support themselves. This cultural shift maps well onto the larger shift in Korea from a collectivist culture to a more individualized and industrialized nation. Though the United States is itself individualized and industrialized (which means in some ways the United States and Korea have become more similar), the difference here is that many Koreans appear to be struggling to find a balance between older cultural traditions and modernization, whereas the United States has been an individualist nation from the beginning. Individualism does not represent a conflict with our cultural identity but stands in stark contrast to recent and historic cultural tendencies in Korea. Older adults are not as honored as they were and must fend for themselves. The expectations for success in school and career are so intense that anything short of perfection may be viewed as irreparably damaging. There is also a sense within Korean culture that discussing distress and mental illness is a sign of weakness, a belief that increases stigma and shame and diminishes social connections.[23,24]

Taken together, Japan and South Korea are two countries that have worked hard to diminish access to firearms. Though the measures taken by these nations were not truly suicide prevention efforts, they nonetheless addressed suicide means, so they are relevant to our discussion. Undoubtedly the lack of access to guns in Japan and

South Korea has prevented some individuals from dying by suicide there, just as bridge barriers have prevented some individuals from dying by suicide in the United States. Because guns were never prominently represented in suicide deaths in Japan and South Korea, however, their removal from the marketplace of suicide methods did not impact the national rate, just as remarkably effective bridge barriers do not measurably reduce the suicide rate in the United States (but absolutely save lives).

Means safety hinges upon the decreased access to or lethality of commonly used highly lethal methods for suicide, and which methods are common depend on many things, including cultural variables such as those discussed above. In the United States, guns play a prominent role in suicide nationally. The fact that they are not prominent in other countries simply means that what works for one culture and country will not necessarily work as well for others—just as what motivates one group of individuals to seek mental health care may not for others (what is appealing about mental health care to an adolescent female may be perceived as uncomfortable by an older adult male military veteran, for instance). Culture, perspective, and comfort and familiarity with specific means are vital here. Furthermore, although far from perfect, the availability of mental health treatment in the United States far surpasses that of Japan and South Korea, a sign that U.S. suicide prevention efforts largely address suicidal desire while failing to address capability—while the opposite is true across the Pacific (although admittedly, suicide prevention efforts in Asia likely are not overtly conceptualized as addressing the capability for suicide, which is a Western concept).

Why Should a Bad Choice by Someone Else Infringe Upon the Constitutional Rights of Others?

The third and final argument against means safety that I will address here rests on the notion that means safety efforts represent an undue burden on the constitutional rights of law abiding citizens, inflicted upon them due to the bad decisions of a select few. This perspective, as far as I can tell, is generally borne of fears that means safety would undermine the Second Amendment. For those for whom gun access is a meaningful part of their cultural identities, I see how this could be threatening. My concern with this perspective is twofold, however. First, nothing that I have promoted throughout this book has entailed a single change to the Second Amendment. I made this claim in the introduction, and I meant it: I have no desire to alienate or villainize anyone, and my suggestions are not intended to cause harm. The means safety measures I support involve caution and safety, not the systematic removal of guns by an outside force seeking to eliminate gun ownership. Do I think the world would be safer and suicide would be much less common if guns were eliminated? Absolutely. It would be difficult to overstate how certain I am about this. I also realize, however, that guns are not going anywhere, and I do not wish to waste the opportunity that this book represents by proposing unreasonable measures that would be summarily rejected by the very people we need the most as active partners in making means safety work: the gun-owning community. The Second Amendment is in no danger from me, and my recommendations need not and will not infringe upon the rights of gun owners.

I also take issue with this perspective because of its rather dismissive characterization of suicide. Although I certainly do not consider suicide to be a "good choice," to dismiss it simply as a bad one is not productive and overlooks the anguish and hopelessness present in the minds and hearts of those who have decided to die, whether by gun or some other method. Those who attempt or die by suicide are not to be viewed as an inconvenience to the cause of gun rights or as a fringe group that makes guns seem more dangerous than they really are. The pain so apparent in suicide notes should quickly make clear the agony suicidal individuals are experiencing when they make the decision to die. They are fellow Americans, neighbors, friends, teachers, and they deserve compassion, not scorn.

Those who die by suicide using a gun are not so unlike those who own guns but who never contemplate suicide. As of now, we are not effective at identifying ahead of time those who will and will not pick up a gun and kill themselves. This is because so many of the clues that people think will reveal to us who is vulnerable simply do not do so with any specificity. At the end of the day, suicide decedents are not as different from us as most people seem to think, and the variables that we think tell us about who is at risk—depression, difficulties regulating emotions, and many more—provide little to no information regarding who is likely to attempt suicide and who will only think about it.[25] This is not an "us" and "them" situation in which suicidal people are different than we are and in need of fundamentally different rules and protections. Suicide affects all of us, and we often remain unaware that someone is struggling with suicidal thoughts until he is dead. At any given moment, your neighbor, friend, family member, or partner may very well be having these thoughts and simply not telling you. As hard as it might be to imagine right now, you yourself may experience these thoughts in the future. This is why our prevention tools must address the possibility that suicide risk is nearby, perhaps even in our homes. Any other approach—any assumption that suicide affects "them" and not "us"—will fail to truly reduce risk.

It is not unlikely that many who have died by suicide spent much of their lives believing that they could never kill themselves and that they were somehow fundamentally different from those who would do so. But we are all vulnerable to thoughts of suicide and suicidal actions under the right conditions—whether we own a gun or not. The fact is that those who do own a gun are more vulnerable to actually dying by suicide. That's the point. We are not even particularly good at guessing if we ourselves will die this way in the future, so our ability to guess this about others—at least without a strong understanding of what research is telling us about factors that predict future suicidal behavior—is remarkably limited.

Despite great advances in scientific and medical research, in the year 2017 we are no better at predicting who will die by suicide and who will not than we were in the 1950s.[26] So we are left with two options. We can continue to fail to reduce our suicide rate by limiting gun-related suicide prevention efforts to those *we think* are at risk, or we can expand our efforts and shift the tone of the conversation in a way that promotes safety among gun owners on a broader scale. The first option is ineffective at saving lives, whereas the second infringes on not much of anything and offers us a chance to prevent more deaths. To me, the choice is simple.

Conclusion

I WROTE THIS BOOK WITH A SENSE OF URGENCY. SUICIDE IS an undeniable public health crisis in America, and yet it is an enormous task to even get people to talk about it. Systemic change geared toward truly effective suicide prevention requires much more than that, so at times optimism is elusive for me. All this being said, I do not want to misrepresent the landscape of suicide prevention and imply that there is no reason for hope, nor signs of progress. The community of suicide researchers is a small one, so I have had the pleasure of getting to know many of the individuals out there pushing us forward with research. I am continually impressed with the passion and brilliance that propels their work and their ability to shape the way I think about this problem. Investment in this work will undoubtedly result in many lives saved.

So my sense of urgency does not stem from a worry that everything we are doing is wrong or that the work my fellow researchers and I are doing is valueless. Rather, it stems from the understanding that we are missing opportunities to be more effective at prevention and that guns represent a central component of that issue. We cannot simply keep doing what we have been doing and hope for the best.

One promising development that has inspired me recently is the campaign by the American Foundation for Suicide Prevention

(AFSP) to reduce the national suicide rate by 20% by 2025. When it launched this initiative, the AFSP called for research proposals for "big ideas"—not simple continuation of standard prevention research in need of new funding but rather paradigm shifting approaches that engage diverse groups in an effort to produce tangible effects on the rate at which people die by suicide. It's not a moonshot, but this is a concerted effort on the part of a prominent suicide prevention group to motivate a different type of work better positioned to accomplish the primary goal of suicide prevention. Within the scope of this general campaign, AFSP recently announced a partnership with the National Shooting Sports Foundation (NSSF) for a pilot project that will launch in four states—Alabama, Kentucky, Missouri, and New Mexico—and will build off some of the work by Cathy Barber in New Hampshire that I discussed earlier in the book.[1] The stated goal for this particular project, which represents only one component of the 20% by 2025 initiative, is to prevent approximately 10,000 suicides over the next decade. The basic structure of the project involves the development of education materials on suicide risk and the promotion of safe storage and voluntary and temporary removal of firearms from the home during times of risk. The NSSF will promote the campaign widely, using materials that it helped develop alongside suicide prevention experts. The materials will be integrated into training curriculums by shooting range operators and various gun safety instructors, thereby placing suicide prevention alongside accident prevention in firearms training.

There are many aspects of this project that I admire and several of the plans align well with my suggestions from chapter 7. The collaboration between suicide prevention experts and the gun-owning community has enormous implications, as it facilitates a conversation that has historically been difficult to maintain, and it greatly enhances the credibility of the message. The integration of suicide prevention into firearms safety courses helps ensure that suicide is a topic that gun owners discuss and plan for just as they do with accidents. The focus on gun owners also increases the odds that the message of suicide prevention will reach men. As I stated numerous times throughout this book, men represent a large majority of suicide deaths in America, but they tend to avoid our mental healthcare system. Suicide prevention has, in some ways, been geared more consistently toward women even though suicide disproportionately affects men. This project reaches out in a way that is more likely to resonate with men, and in that sense, it might open the door for some who would have never sought help.

In the absence of a buyback program such as Australia's that would greatly diminish the number of guns in our country, or the establishment of legislation that prevents future sales, it is a safe assumption that our country will remain inundated with guns in a way that sets it apart from every other country in the world. Given this, some of our best opportunities to prevent suicide are going to involve minimizing the risk posed by a gun that is already present rather than limiting the acquisition of a gun in the first place. The AFSP/NSSF project will serve as an important first step in testing that possibility.

I would be remiss if I did not also express a concern I have with the way that means safety among gun owners is currently concep-tualized. This concern is somewhat abstract, but I think it may prove important in determining how and when to pursue specific aspects of firearms-related means safety. In mid-2016, Thomas Joiner and Ian Stanley published a paper in *Psychiatry* that proposed that the behavior of individuals in a suicidal crisis could potentially be under-stood as a parallel to how other species respond to predatory threat[2]. In other words, a suicidal person exhibits some behaviors and phys-iological responses that are similar to what many animals (includ-ing humans) display when they feel they are about to be attacked or killed. At first glance, that idea might seem farfetched, but Joiner and Stanley made several compelling points. A mix of scientific studies and clinical lore has noted that in the moments and hours before people die by suicide, they tend to exhibit both overarousal (agita-tion, irritability, nightmares, insomnia) and withdrawal (social with-drawal, cessation of eating, cessation of drinking among chronic daily drinkers). These two processes—overarousal and "shutdown"—are in many ways contradictory, but in this particular circumstance, they co-occur quite often. The authors here noted that when ani-mals sense that there is a predator nearby, they exhibit many of these same characteristics. They will stop eating, increase their vigilance, literally sleep with one eye open if they are positioned in the outer area of a defensive arrangement within their pack, and experience acute physiological changes that facilitate fighting or fleeing from an enemy. The question then becomes whether suicidal crises mirror this process and whether we can reasonably consider such individuals as feeling as though somebody is about to try to kill them (with the fact that they themselves are their own killers being almost irrelevant).

This idea is purely theoretical, so I do not want to dig too deeply into it, but when I read the article it made me wonder: if, in the moments and hours leading up to death by suicide, people experience physiological responses similar to responses to predatory threat, is it reasonable to expect that we can convince them to give up their guns, as the ASFP/NSSP project would have them do? In other words, are means safety efforts as currently designed asking people to give up perhaps their most powerful perceived source of "protection" in a moment of extreme perceived threat? Though the gun is the very thing that will cause their own deaths, people have shown a remarkably strong resistance to the notion that guns are more dangerous than helpful when kept nearby in times of threat and potential confusion.[3,4] If my concerns are valid (and they may not be), it would underscore the importance of enacting means safety efforts much earlier in the progression of suicide risk. Asking individuals at imminent risk for suicide to give up their guns would, in this scenario, likely prompt either overt or covert refusal (perhaps surrendering one gun while keeping secret the fact that he or she owns another that will be used instead). Given recently published evidence that 3% of the nation owns half of America's guns,[5] it is not unlikely that a gun owner owns more than one firearm and that a willingness to give up or shift the storage practices of one gun would fail to address the entirety of that individual's arsenal. My point here is not that means safety is a problematic idea, but that as we think about when and how to implement it, we need to keep in mind that the willingness of the gun owner to engage in such practices might shift at different levels of risk.

In a randomized controlled trial called Project Safe Guard that I will launch in late 2017 with my colleagues Dan Capron, Craig Bryan, and AnnaBelle Bryan, we will build on this notion by administering a single session of firearm-specific means safety counseling with U.S. National Guard soldiers. Importantly, we will not be recruiting soldiers specifically based on their behavior or on any statement that they are experiencing thoughts of suicide. Instead, we are recruiting soldiers in a high-risk demographic group (male soldiers under age 30 who own a personal firearm) and planning ahead for crises that might never come. Our sense is that if we wait for these individuals to tell us they are at risk, we will fail to help them, as soldiers tend to underreport such issues. Additionally, based on Joiner and Stanley's idea, if we wait until the crisis is already in full force, the soldiers may be unwilling to engage.

The results of projects like this are not yet known. They may prove illuminating and provide us with clear guidelines on what to do to address firearm suicides—or they might yield very little in actionable information. That is the way of life in science, which is one of the reasons why it is so important to have several independent groups conducting separate trials at the same time. We learn more about important issues when we study them intensely and broadly than we do when we put all of our efforts into a single project. Here is where I think there should be a strong sense of agreement between people like me, who favor broadly implemented means safety-focused suicide prevention efforts, and those who prioritize individual freedom and the minimization of broadly implemented laws and regulations. Members of the latter group have historically resisted federal action because they view the independence of states as pivotal, and indeed have referred to states as the individual laboratories of the nation. If states are laboratories, then this is their opportunity to demonstrate what works. In a sense, that is what the AFSP/NSSF project represents, but I think the idea could be taken much further. We cannot randomly assign states to have or not have specific legislation, and I understand the political implications of high-gun-ownership states enacting legislation that may appear liberal and threatening to gun ownership, but if we truly want to understand what works at what time and for which individuals, we need states to be willing to at least temporarily try out a variety of approaches. You cannot be a laboratory if you are unwilling to test new ideas.

Wrapping Up

As I conclude this section we are in the final days of September, which annually serves as National Suicide Prevention Month. In some ways, I see a lot of value in National Suicide Prevention Month. There is certainly nothing to lose in increasing awareness of an important issue that is too often ignored, and I think that a lot of people—those who have survived attempts or lost someone to suicide, for example—who tend to feel marginalized and ashamed experience a sense of relief and community during these weeks.

At the same time, and I realize this likely comes across as somewhat counterintuitive given that I am a suicide researcher trying to increase awareness about suicide, my general impression of National Suicide Prevention Month is that is has almost no value. For generations, mental health treatments were limited by what is known as the "insight fallacy," which is the mistaken belief that understanding something will change it. Individuals suffering from mental illness spent years with therapists trying to uncover the hidden sources of their struggles, as though identifying the culprit would bring them relief today. More recently, even though evidence-based psychological treatments are far from universally practiced, we have studied treatments quite a bit and found that although trying to understand where something came from is interesting and an entirely reasonable impulse, true change is the result of active steps made towards fixing the situation—not of understanding its origins.

National Suicide Prevention Month seems weighed down by the insight fallacy. I want people to know that suicide is a problem, but suicide will not be prevented simply by letting people know how often it happens and who it affects. I like to see people expressing support for those affected by suicide, but posting videos of oneself on Facebook doing 22 pushups in support of veteran suicide prevention will not keep any struggling veterans alive. Efforts such as this are often less about preventing suicide and more about letting people see you talking about preventing suicide. It is a show rather than a concerted effort to change a tragic outcome. This does not diminish the kindness that drives the behavior, but it certainly highlights the limited value of hollow and time-limited action.

We do not need a National Suicide Prevention Month. We need a suicide prevention movement that lasts year round and is relentless in its promotion of practical steps people can take to prevent suicide. The media must drastically increase its coverage of suicide, ensuring that the scope of the problem is emphasized without resulting to sensationalism and stigmatizing word choices (for instance, using pejorative phrases such as "committed suicide" instead of "died by suicide"). Health-care providers should assess patients for suicide risk routinely and systematically and refer those at risk to evidence-based treatments shown through well-designed clinical trials to effectively reduce suicidal thoughts and behaviors. At the governmental level, suicide prevention training should be mandated for health and mental health-care providers (e.g. physicians, social workers), and funding should be made available for simple and effective suicide prevention measures such as bridge barriers. Within the community, everyone should educate themselves about risk factors for suicide, discuss suicide with one another, and remain vigilant for signs of risk in their loved ones.

With respect to firearms, we must have a national conversation about the role of guns in our society, the potential value of limiting access to and slowing down the acquisition process for guns for at least some people, and the importance of safely storing guns and temporarily removing them from the home during times of crisis. Every American should know that most American gun deaths are suicides, and most suicides are gun deaths.

The issue of guns and suicide is an emotional one, weighed down by politics and difficult to engage in for many. We do not have definitive solutions yet to the problem—in part because efforts to obtain them have been actively blocked—but the evidence for means safety focused specifically on guns is compelling. The task that remains before us is to take that knowledge, expand upon it, and implement it in the real world in such a way as to actually save lives and reverse the decade-plus trend of annually increasing suicide rates. We as a nation can no longer ignore the fact that over 40,000 Americans die by suicide every single year. The issue enjoys very little attention or funding; our continued inaction is inexcusable.

As you consider the arguments I put forth in this book, whatever your background and whatever your position on the relationship between suicide and firearms in the United States, I ask that you be willing to talk about it and to consider solutions that reflect what we know about suicide. We will never eliminate this problem entirely, but informed efforts toward suicide prevention, guided by science and a willingness to put personal agendas aside in the pursuit of saving lives, would make this country a better place. It would spare thousands of men, women, and children from the debilitating grief of losing a loved one to suicide.

Notes

Introduction

1. http://www.breitbart.com/big-government/2016/01/05/
   obama-admits-two-thirds-scary-gun-death-statistics-suicides/

Chapter 1

1. https://www.cdc.gov/mmwr/preview/mmwrhtml/ss6013a1.htm
2. http://webappa.cdc.gov/cgi-bin/broker.exe
3. http://www.nhtsa.gov/About+NHTSA/Press+Releases/2015/
   2014-traffic-deaths-drop-but-2015-trending-higher
4. https://www.start.umd.edu/pubs/START_AmericanTerrorism
   Deaths_FactSheet_Oct2015.pdf
5. http://www.motherjones.com/politics/2012/12/mass-shootings-
   mother-jones-full-data
6. http://www.gunviolencearchive.org/reports
7. These data were compiled from the CDC's WISQARS database,
   available at: http://webappa.cdc.gov/cgi-bin/broker.exe

Chapter 2

1. Joiner, T. E. (2011). *Myths about suicide*. Cambridge, MA: Harvard University Press.
2. Popper, K. R. (1968). *The logic of scientific discovery*. New York: Harper & Row.
3. Joiner, T. E. (2005). *Why people die by suicide*. Cambridge, MA: Harvard University Press.
4. Joiner, T. E., Hom, M. A., Hagan, C. R., & Silva, C. (2016). Suicide as a derangement of the self-sacrificial aspect of eusociality. *Psychological Review, 123,* 235–254.
5. Coyne, J. C. (1976). Depression and the response of others. *Journal of Abnormal Psychology, 85,* 186–193.
6. Hammen, C. (1991). Generation of stress in the course of unipolar depression. *Journal of Abnormal Psychology, 100,* 555–561.
7. Cuijpers, P., van Straten, A., & Warmerdam, L. (2007). Behavioral activiation treatments of depression: A meta-analysis. *Clinical Psychology Review, 27,* 318–326.
8. Linehan, M. M., Comtois, K. A., Murray, A. M., Brown, M. Z., Gallop, R. J., & Heard, H., et al. (2006). Two-year randomized controlled trial and follow-up of dialectical behavior therapy vs therapy by experts for suicidal behaviors and borderline personality disorder. *Archives of General Psychiatry, 63,* 757–766.
9. Weissman, M. M, Klerman, G. L., Prusoff, B. A., Sholomskas, D., & Padian, N. (1981). Depressed outpatients. Results one year after treatment with drugs and/or interpersonal psychotherapy. *Archives of General Psychiatry, 38,* 51–55.
10. Motto, J. A., & Bostrom, A. G. (2001). A randomized controlled trial of postcrisis suicide prevention. *Psychiatric Services, 52,* 828–833.
11. Joiner, T. E., Hollar, D., & Van Orden, K. (2006). On Buckeyes, Gators, Super Bowl Sunday, and the Miracle on Ice: "Pulling together" is associated with lower suicide rates. *Journal of Social and Personality Psychology, 25,* 179–195.
12. For a summary of such evidence, see this description by the CDC: http://www.cdc.gov/violenceprevention/suicide/holiday.html
13. Van Orden, K. A., Witte, T. K., Gordon, K. H., Bender, T. W., & Joiner, T. E. (2008). Suicidal desire and the capability for

suicide: Tests of the interpersonal-psychological theory of suicidal behavior among adults. *Journal of Consulting and Clinical Psychology, 76,* 72–83.

14. Anestis, M. D., Khazem, L. R., Mohn, R. S., & Green, B. A. (2015). Testing the main hypotheses of the interpersonal-psychological theory of suicidal behavior in a large diverse sample of United States military personnel. *Comprehensive Psychiatry, 60,* 78–85.

15. Baumeister, R. F. (1990). Suicide as escape from self. *Psychological Review, 97,* 90–113.

16. Owens, D., Horrocks, J., & House, A. (2002). Fatal and non-fatal repetition of self-harm: Systematic review. *British Journal of Psychiatry, 181,* 193–199.

17. Joiner, T. E., Walker, R. L., Rudd, M. D., & Jobes, D. A. (1999). Scientizing and routinizing the assessment of suicidality in outpatient practice. *Professional Psychology: Research and Practice, 30,* 447–453.

18. Bryan, C. J., Cukrowicz, K. C., West, C. L., & Morrow, C. E. (2010). Combat experience and the acquired capability for suicide. *Journal of Clinical Psychology, 66,* 1044–1056.

19. Franklin, J. C., Hessel, E. T., & Prinstein, M. J. (2011). Clarifying the role of pain tolerance in suicidal capability. *Psychiatry Research, 189,* 362–367.

20. Smith, A. R., Ribeiro, J. D., Mikolajewski, A., Taylor, J., Joiner, T. E., & Iacono, W. G. (2012). An examination of environmental and genetic contributions to the determinants of suicidal behavior among male twins. *Psychiatry Research, 197,* 60–65.

21. Anestis, M. D., Khazem, L. R., Mohn, R. S., & Green, B. A. (2015). Testing the main hypotheses of the interpersonal-psychological theory of suicidal behavior in a large diverse sample of United States military personnel. *Comprehensive Psychiatry, 60,* 78–85.

22. Joiner, T. E., Van Orden, K. A., Witte, T. K., Selby, E. A., Riberio, J. D., Lewis, R., & Rudd, M. D. (2009). Main predictions of the interpersonal-psychological theory of suicidal behavior: Empirical tests in two samples of young adults. *Journal of Abnormal Psychology, 118,* 634–646.

23. Anestis, M. D., Soberay, K. A., Gutierrez, P. M., Hernandez, T. D., & Joiner, T. E. (2014). Reconsidering the link between impulsivity and suicidal behavior. *Personality and Social Psychology Review, 18,* 366–386.

24. Anestis, M. D., Pennings, S. M., & Williams, T. J. (2014). Preliminary results from an examination of episodic planning in suicidal behavior. *Crisis: The Journal of Crisis Intervention and Suicide Prevention, 35,* 186–192.

Chapter 3

1. Simon, R. (2007). Gun safety management with patients at risk for suicide. *Suicide and Life-Threatening Behavior, 37,* 518–526.
2. Brent, D. A. (2001). Firearms and suicide. *Annals of the New York Academy of Science, 932,* 225–240.
3. Wintemute, J. G., Parham, C. A., Beaumont, J. J., Wright, M., & Drake, C. (1999). Mortality among recent purchasers of handguns. *New England Journal of Medicine, 341,* 1583–1589.
4. Conwell, Y., Duberstein, P. R., Connor, K., Eberly, S., Cox, C., & Caine, E. D. (2002). Access to firearms and risk for suicide in middle-aged and older adults. *American Journal of Geriatric Psychiatry, 10*(4), 407–416.
5. Hamilton, D., & Kposowa, A. J. (2015). Firearms and violent death in the United States: Gun ownership, gun control, and mortality rates in 16 states, 2005–2009. *British Journal of Education, Society & Behavioural Science, 7,* 84–98.
6. Hemenway, D., & Miller, M. (2002). Association of rates of household handgun ownership, lifetime major depression, and serious suicidal thoughts with rates of suicide across US census regions. *Injury Prevention, 8*(4), 313–316.
7. Kellermann, A. L., Rivara, F. P., Somes, G., Reay, D. T., Francisco, J., Banton, J. G., . . . & Hackman, B. B. (1992). Suicide in the home in relation to gun ownership. *New England Journal of Medicine, 327*(7), 467–472.
8. Miller, M., Hemenway, D., & Azrael, D. (2004). Firearms and suicide in the northeast. *Journal of Trauma and Acute Care Surgery, 57*(3), 626–632.
9. Miller, M., Lippmann, S. J., Azrael, D., & Hemenway, D. (2007). Household firearm ownership and rates of suicide across the 50 United States. *Journal of Trauma and Acute Care Surgery, 62*(4), 1029–1035.
10. Miller, M., Barber, C., White, R. A., & Azrael, D. (2013). Firearms and suicide in the United States: Is risk independent of underlying

suicidal behavior?. *American Journal of Epidemiology, 178*(6), 946–955.

11. Miller, M., Warren, M., Hemenway, D., & Azrael, D. (2015). Firearms and suicide in US cities. *Injury Prevention, 21*(e1), e116–e119.

12. Opoliner, A., Azrael, D., Barber, C., Fitzmaurice, G., Miller, M. (2014). Explaining geographic patterns of suicide in the US: The role of firearms and antidepressants. *Injury Epidemiology, 1*(6). https://injepijournal.springeropen.com/articles/10.1186/2197-1714-1-6

13. Kim, N., Mickelson, J. B., Brenner, B. E., Haws, C. A., Yurgelun-Todd, D. A., & Renshaw, P. F. (2011). Altitude, gun ownership, rural areas, and suicide. *American Journal of Psychiatry, 168,* 49–54.

14. Anestis, M. D., & Houtsma, C. (in press). The association between gun ownership and statewide overall suicide rates. *Suicide and Life-Threatening Behavior.*

15. Non-suicidal self-injury (NSSI) is the intentional infliction of physical harm to oneself without the intent to die. Although related to suicide, this behavior is distinct in many ways—how quickly it emerges, what methods are used, why people engage in the behavior, etc.—and as such including NSSI in a tally of suicide attempts is fairly problematic.

16. http://www.smallarmssurvey.org/fileadmin/docs/A-Yearbook/2007/en/full/Small-Arms-Survey-2007-Chapter-02-EN.pdf

17. Kalesan, B., Villarreal, M. D., Keyes, K. M., & Galea, S. (2016). Gun ownership and social gun culture. *Injury Prevention, 22,* 216–220. Available online at: http://injuryprevention.bmj.com/content/early/2015/06/09/injuryprev-2015-041586.abstract

18. Anestis, M. D., & Capron, D. W. (in press). Deadly experience: The association between firing a gun and various aspects of suicide risk. *Suicide and Life-Threatening Behavior.*

Chapter 4

1. http://www.cnn.com/2015/08/27/politics/donald-trump-virginia-shooting-mental-health-gun-laws/

2. http://www.cnn.com/2016/01/12/politics/state-of-the-union-gun-control-empty-seat/

3. Bertolote, J. M., & Fleischmann, A. (2002). Suicide and psychiatric diagnosis: A worldwide perspective. *World Psychiatry, 1,* 181–185.

4. Thomas Joiner is one prominent advocate for this viewpoint, and his lab is currently investigating the potential utility of a construct they refer to as Acute Suicidal Affective Disturbance (ASAD) that would largely account for the additional 10%.

5. Kessler, R. C., Berglund, P., Demler, O., Jin, R., Koretz, D., Merikangas, K. R., et al. (2003). The epidemiology of major depressive disorder: Results from the National Comorbidity Survey Replication (NCS-R). *JAMA, 289,* 3095–3105.

6. http://www.diabetes.org/diabetes-basics/statistics/

7. http://www.cdc.gov/hiv/statistics/overview/

8. Robins, E., Murphy, G. E., Wilkerson, R. H., Gassner, S., & Kayes, J. (1959). Some clinical considerations in the prevention of suicide based on a study of 134 successful suicides. *American Journal of Public Health, 49,* 888–898.

9. Borges, G., Angst, J., Nock, M. K., Ruscio, A. M., & Kessler, R. C. (2008). Risk factors for the incidence and persistence of suicide-related outcomes: A 10-year follow-up study using the National Comorbidity Surveys. *Journal of Affective Disorders, 105,* 25–33.

10. Van Orden et al. (2010) review paper

11. Linehan, M. M. (1993). *Cognitive behavioral treatment of borderline personality disorder.* New York: Guilford.

12. Kliem, S., Kroger, C., & Kosfelder, J. (2010). Dialectical behavior therapy for borderline personality disorder: A meta-analysis using mixed-effects modeling. *Journal of Consulting and Clinical Psychology, 78,* 936–951.

13. Linehan, M. M., Korslund, K. E., Harned, M. S., Gallop, R. J., Lungu, A., Neacsiu, A. D., . . . Murray-Gregory, A. M. (2015). Dialectical behavior therapy for high suicide risk in individuals with borderline personality disorder: A randomized clinical trial and component analysis. *JAMA Psychiatry, 72,* 475–482.

14. Rudd, M. D. (2012). Brief cognitive behavioral therapy (BCBT) for suicidality in military populations. *Military Psychology, 24,* 592–603.

15. Rudd, M. D., Bryan, C. J., Wertenberger, E. G., Peterson, A. L., Young-McCaughan, S., Mintz, J., . . . & Bruce, T. O. (2015). Brief

cognitive-behavioral therapy effects on post-treatment suicide attempts in a military sample: Results of a randomized clinical trial with 2-year follow-up. *American Journal of Psychiatry, 172,* 441–449.

16. Data derived from the National Cancer Institute. Retrieved from http://seer.cancer.gov/statfacts/html/lungb.html

17. Data derived from the Insurance Institute for Highway Safety and the Highway Loss Data Institute. Retrieved from http://www.iihs.org/iihs/topics/t/general-statistics/fatalityfacts/state-by-state-overview/2013

18. All of these data were derived from the Centers for Disease Control and Prevention's Web-based Injury Statistics Query and Reporting System (WISQARS). Retrieved from http://www.cdc.gov/injury/wisqars/index.html

19. Alabas, O. A., Tashani, O. A., Tabasam, G., & Johnson, M. I. (2012). Gender role affects experimental pain responses: A systematic review with meta-analysis. *European Journal of Pain, 16,* 1211–1223.

20. Witte, T. K., Gordon, K. H., Smith, P. N., & Van Orden, K. A. (2012). Stoicism and sensation seeking: Male vulnerabilities for the acquired capability for suicide. *Journal of Research in Personality, 46,* 384–392.

21. Bryan, C. J., Morrow, C. E., Anestis, M. D., & Joiner, T. E. (2010). A preliminary test of the interpersonal-psychological theory of suicidal behavior in a military sample. *Personality and Individual Differences, 48,* 347–350.

22. Assavedo, B. L., & Anestis, M. D. (in press). Military personnel compared to multiple suicide attempters: Interpersonal theory of suicide constructs. *Death Studies.*

23. Granato, S. L., Smith, P. N., & Selwyn, C. N. (2015). Acquired capability and masculine gender norm adherence: Potential pathways to higher rates of male suicide. *Psychology of Men and Masculinity, 16,* 246–253.

24. Kalesan, B., Villarreal, M. D., Keyes, K. M., & Galea, S. (2016). Gun ownership and social gun culture. *Injury Prevention, 22,* 216–220. doi:10.1136/injuryprev-2015-041586

25. Kessler, R. C., Brown, R. L., & Broman, C. L. (1981). Sex differences in psychiatric help-seeking: Evidence from four large-scale surveys. *Journal of Health and Social Behavior, 22,* 49–64.

26. Duberstein, P. R., Conwell, Y., Seidlitz, L., Lyness, J. M., Cox, C., & Caine, E. D. (1999). Age and suicidal ideation in older depressed inpatients. *American Journal of Geriatric Psychiatry, 7*, 289–296.

27. Cukrowicz, K. C., Jahn, D. R., Graham, R. D., Poindexter, E. K., & Williams, R. B. (2013). Suicide risk in older adults: Evaluating models of risk and predicting excess zeros in a primary care sample. *Journal of Abnormal Psychology, 122*, 1021–1030.

28. Bryan, C. J., & Morrow, C. E. (2011). Circumventing mental health stigma by embracing the warrior culture: Lessons learned from the Defender's Edge program. *Professional Psychology: Research and Practice, 42*, 16–23.

29. Pietrzak, R. H., Johnson, D. C., Goldstein, M. B., Malley, J. C., & Southwick, S. M. (2009). Psychological resilience and post-deployment social support protect against traumatic stress and depressive symptoms in soldiers returning from Operations Enduring Freedom and Iraqi Freedom. *Depression and Anxiety, 26*, 745–751.

30. Kim, P. Y., Britt, T. W., Klocko, R. P., Riviere, L. A., & Adler, A. B. (2011). Stigma, negative attitudes about treatment, and utilization of mental health care among soldiers. *Military Psychology, 23*, 65–81.

31. Data derived from the Department of Defense Suicide Event Report (DoDSER). Retrieved from http://t2health.dcoe.mil/programs/dodser

32. Anestis, M. D., & Green, B. A. (2015). The impact of varying levels of confidentiality on disclosure of suicidal thoughts in a sample of United States National Guard personnel. *Journal of Clinical Psychology, 71*, 1023–1030.

33. Anestis, M. D., & Bryan, C. J. (2013). Means and capacity for suicidal behavior: A comparison of the ratio of suicide attempts and deaths by suicide in the US military and general population. *Journal of Affective Disorders, 148*, 42–47.

34. Suokas, J., Suominen, K., Isometsa, E., Ostamo, A., & Lonnqvist, J. (2001). Long-term risk factors for suicide mortality after attempted suicide—findings from a 14-year follow-up study. *Acta Psychiatrica Scandanavica, 104*, 117–121.

35. Chu, C., Klein, K. M., Buchman-Schmitt, J. M., Hom, H. A., Hagan, C. R., & Joiner, T. E. (2015). Routinized assessment of

suicide risk in clinical practice: An empirically informed update. *Journal of Clinical Psychology, 71,* 1186–1200. doi: 10.1002/jclp.22210

36. Anestis, M. D. (2016). Prior suicide attempts are less common in suicide decedents who died by firearms relative to those who died by other means. *Journal of Affective Disorders, 189,* 106–109.

37. Becker, C. B., Zayfert, C., & Anderson, E. (2004). A survey of spychologists' attitudes towards and utilization of exposure therapy for PTSD. *Behavior Research and Therapy, 42,* 277–292.

38. Freheit, S. R., Vye, C., Swan, R., & Cady, M. (2004). Cognitive-behavioral therapy for anxiety: Is dissemination working? *Behavior Therapy, 27,* 25–30.

39. Lilienfeld, S. O., Ritschel, L. A., Lynn, S. J., Brown, A. P., Cautin, R. L., & Latzman, R. D. (2013). The research-practice gap: Bridging the schism between eating disorder researchers and practitioners.

40. Golnik, A. E., & Ireland, M. (2009). Complementary alternative medicine for children with autism: A physician survey. *Journal of Autism and Developmental Disorders, 39,* 996–1005.

41. Anestis, M. D., Anestis, J. C., Zawilinski, L. L., Hopkins, T. A., & Lilienfeld, S. O. (2014). Equine-related treatments for mental illness lack empirical support: A systematic review of empirical investigations. *Journal of Clinical Psychology, 70,* 1115–1132.

Chapter 5

1. Anestis, M. D., Law, K. C., Jin, H., Houtsma, C., Khazem, L. R., & Assavedo, B. L. (in press). Treating the capability for suicide: A vital and understudied frontier in suicide prevention. *Suicide and Life-Threatening Behavior.*

2. Centers for Disease Control and Prevention. (2013). HIV and injection drug use in the United States. Retrieved from http://www.cdc.gov/hiv/risk/substanceuese.html

3. Gottleib, M. S. (2001). AIDS—past and future. *New England Journal of Medicine, 344,* 1788–1791.

4. Heimer, R. (1998). Syringe exchange programs: Lowering the transmission of syringe-borne diseases and beyond. *Public Health Reports, 113,* 67–74.

5. Drucker, E., Lurie, P., Wodak, A., & Alcabes, P. (1998). Measuring harm reduction: The effects of needle and syringe exchange programs and methadone maintenance on the ecology of HIV. *AIDS, 12,* 217–230.

6. Lurie, P., & Reingold, A. (1993). The public health impact of needle exchange programs in the United States and abroad. Retrieved from http://caps.ucsf.edu/uploads/pubs/reports/pdf/NEPReportSummary1993.pdf

7. Normand, J., Vlahov, D., & Moses, L. E. (1995). *Preventing HIV Transmission: The role of sterile needles and bleach.* Washington, DC: The National Academies Press.

8. Des Jarlais, D. C., Marmor, M., Paone, D., Titus, S., & Friedman, S. R. (1996). HIV incidence among injecting drug users in New York City syringe-exchange programmes. *Lancet, 348,* 987–991.

9. Hurley, S. F., Jolley, D. J., & Kaldor, J. M. (1997). Effectiveness of needle-exchange programmes for prevention of HIV infection. *Lancet, 349,* 1797–1800.

10. Hall, H. I., Song, R., Rhodes, P., et al. (2008). HIV incidence surveillance group. Estimation of HIV incidence in the United States. *JAMA, 300,* 520–529.

11. Stanley, I. H., Hom, M. A., Rogers, M. L., Anestis, M. D., & Joiner, T. E. (2016). Discussing firearm ownership and access as part of suicide risk assessment and prevention: 'Means safety' versus 'means restriction.' *Archives of Suicide Research, 21,* 237–253.

12. National Cancer Institute. SEER Stat Fact Sheets: Lung and bronchus cancer. Retrieved from http://seer.cancer.gov/statfacts/html/lungb.html

13. Eheman, C., Henley, S. J., Ballard-Barbash, R., Jacobs, E. J., Schymura, M. J., Noone, A. M., . . .Edward, B. K. (2012). Annual report to the nation on the status of cancer, 1976-2008, Featuring cancers associated with excess weight and lack of sufficient physical activity. *Cancer, 118,* 2338–2366.

14. A brief summary of a book on this topic by these authors can be found at http://www.ncbi.nlm.nih.gov/books/NBK12903/

15. Kreitman, N. (1976). The coal gas story. United Kingdom suicide rates, 1960-71. *British Journal of Preventative and Social Medicine, 30,* 86–93.

16. Bennewith, O., Nowers, M., & Gunnell, D. (2007). Effect of barriers on the Clifton suspension bridge, England, on local patterns of suicide: Implications for prevention. *British Journal of Psychiatry, 190,* 266–267.

17. Bautrais, A .L., Bigg, S. J., Fergusson, D. M., Horwood, L. J., & Larkin, G. L. (2009). Removing bridge barriers stimulates suicides: An unfortunate natural experiment. *Australian and New Zealand Journal of Psychiatry, 43,* 495–497.

18. Law, C. K., Sveticic, J., & de Leo, D. (2014). Restricting access to a suicide hotspot does not shift the problem to another location. An experiment of two river bridges in Brisbane, Australia. *Australian and New Zealand Journal of Public Health, 38,* 134–138.

19. Pirkis, J., Too, L. S., Spittal, M. J., Krysinska, K., Robinson, J., & Cheung, Y. T. D. (2015). Interventions to reduce suicides at suicide hotspots: A systematic review and meta-analysis. *Lancet Psychiatry, 2,* 994–1001.

Chapter 6

1. Boyd, J. H. (1983). The increasing rate of suicide by firearms. *New England Journal of Medicine, 308,* 872–874.

2. Lester, D., & Murrell, M. E. (1980). The influence of gun control laws on suicidal behavior. *American Journal of Psychiatry, 137,* 121–122.

3. Lester, D. & Murrell, M. E. (1982). The preventative effect of strict gun control laws on suicide and homicide. *Suicide and Life-Threatening Behavior, 12,* 131–140.

4. Lester, D., & Murrell, M. E. (1986). The influence of gun control laws on personal violence. *Journal of Community Psychology, 14,* 315–318.

5. Lester, D. (1987). Availability of guns and the likelihood of suicide. *Sociology and Social Research, 71,* 287–288.

6. Loftin, C., McDowall, D., Wiersema, B., & Cottey, T. J. (1991). Effects of restrictive licensing of handguns on homicide and suicide in the District of Columbia. *New England Journal of Medicine, 325,* 1615–1620.

7. Rich, C. L., Young, J. G., Fowler, R. C., Wagner, J., & Black, N. A. (1990). Guns and suicide: Possible effects of some specific legislation. *American Journal of Psychiatry, 147,* 342–346.

8. Carrington, P. J., & Moyer, S. (1994). Gun control and suicide in Ontario. *American Journal of Psychiatry, 151*, 606–608.

9. Conner, K. R., & Zhong, Y. (2003). State firearm laws and rates of suicide in men and women. *American Journal of Preventative Medicine, 25*, 320–324.

10. Price, J. H., Thompson, A. J., & Dake, J. A. (2004). Factors associated with state variations in homicide, suicide, and unintentional firearm deaths. *Journal of Community Health, 29*, 271–283.

11. Fleegler, E. W., Lee, L. K., Monuteaux, M. C., Hemenway, D., & Mannix, R. (2013). Firearm legislation and firearm-related fatalities in the United States. *JAMA Internal Medicine, 173*, 732–740.

12. The Brady Center's website is http://www.bradycampaign.org/

13. Ludwig, J., & Cook, P. J. (2000). Homicide and suicide rates associated with the implementation of the Brady Handgun Violence Prevention Act. *JAMA, 284*, 585–591.

14. Sumner, S. A., Layde, P. M., & Guse, C. E. (2008). Firearm death rates and association with level of firearm purchase background check. *American Journal of Preventative Medicine, 35*, 1–6.

15. You can access the site at (https://www.nraila.org/) and search by state for this information.

16. Anestis, M. D., Khazem, L. R., Law, K. C., Houtsma, C., LeTard, R., Moberg, F., & Martin, R. (2015). The association between state laws regulating handgun ownership and suicide rates. *American Journal of Public Health, 105*, 2059–2067.

17. Anestis, M. D., & Anestis, J. C. (2015). Suicide rates and statewide laws regulating access and exposure to handguns. *American Journal of Public Health, 105*, 2049–2058.

18. Anestis, M. D., & Capron, D. W. (2016). The associations between state veteran population rates, handgun legislation, and statewide suicide rates. *Journal of Psychiatric Research, 74*, 30–34.

19. Anestis, M. D., Anestis, J. C., & Butterworth, S. E. (2017). Handgun legislation and changes in statewide overall suicide rates. *American Journal of Public Health, 107*, 579–581.

20. Lubin, G., Werbeloff, N., Halperin, D., Shmushkevitch, M., Weiser, M., & Knobler, H. (2010). Decrease in suicide rates after a change of policy reducing access to firearms in adolescents: A naturalistic epidemiological study. *Suicide and Life-Threatening Behavior, 40*, 421–424.

Chapter 7

1. http://www.madd.org/about-us/
2. A concise history of the Ad Council efforts on Drunk Driving and corresponding traffic fatality data can be found at http://www.abso-luteadvocacy.org/drunk-driving-prevention-media-campaigns/
3. http://www.adcouncil.org/Our-Campaigns/The-Classics/Drunk-Driving-Prevention
4. http://www.adcouncil.org/Our-Campaigns/Safety/Buzzed-Driving-Prevention
5. A summary of traffic fatalities (1994-2013) in the US can be found at http://www-fars.nhtsa.dot.gov/Main/reportslinks.aspx - Similar data for 1982-1994 can be found at http://www-nrd.nhtsa.dot.gov/Pubs/FARS94.pdf
6. http://www.hsph.harvard.edu/means-matter/downloads/
7. Joiner, T. E., & Stanley, I. H . (2016). Can the phenomenology of a suicidal crisis be usefully understood as a suite of antipredator defensive reactions? *Psychiatry, 79,* 107–119.
8. Robins, E. (1981). *The final months: A study of the lives of 134 persons who committed suicide.* Oxford: Oxford University Press.
9. Ilgen, M. A., Zivin, K., McCammon, R. J., & Valenstein, M. (2008). Mental illness, previous suicidality, and access to guns in the United States. *Psychiatric Services, 59,* 198–200.
10. Khazem, L. R., Houtsma, C., Gratz, K. L., Tull, M. T., & Anestis, M. D. (2016). Firearms matter: The moderating role of firearm storage in the association between current suicidal ideation and likelihood of future suicide attempts among United States military personnel. *Military Psychology, 28,* 25–33.
11. Miller, M., Barber, C., Azrael, D., Hemenway, D., & Molnar, B. E. (2009). Recent psychopathology, suicidal thoughts, and suicide attempts in households with and without firearms: Findings from the National Comordibity Study Replication. *Injury Prevention, 15,* 183–187.
12. Betz, M. E., Barber, C., & Miller, M. (2011). Suicidal behavior and firearm access: Results from the second Injury Control and Risk Survey. *Suicide and Life-Threatening Behavior, 41,* 384–391.
13. https://www.mdwfp.com/education-outreach/hunter-education.aspx

14. Fatal injury numbers can be computed at the state, regional, and national level using the CDC's Web-Based Injury Statistics Query and Reporting System (WISQARS); http://www.cdc.gov/injury/wisqars/fatal.html

15. http://theconnectprogram.org/firearms-safety-coalitions-role-nh-suicide-prevention

16. Vriniotis, M., Barber, C., Frank, E., Demicco, R., & the New Hampshire Firearm Safety Coalition (2015). A suicide prevention campaign for firearm dealers in New Hampshire. *Suicide and Life-Threatening Behavior, 45,* 157–163.

Chapter 8

1. De Moore, G. M., & Robertson, A. R. (1999). Suicide attempts by firearms and by leaping from heights: A comparative study of survivors. *American Journal of Psychiatry, 9,* 1425–1431.

2. Runeson, B., Tidemalm, D., Dahlin, M., Lichtenstein, P., & Langstrom, N. (2010). Method of attempted suicide as a predictor of subsequent successful suicide: National long term cohort study. *British Medical Journal, 340,* c3222.

3. Daigle, M. S. (2005). Suicide prevention through means restriction: Assessing the risk of substitution. A critical review and synthesis. *Accident Analysis and Prevention, 37,* 625–632.

4. Lester, D., & Abe, K. (1989). The effect of restricting access to lethal methods for suicide: A study of suicide by domestic gas in Japan. *Acta Psychiatrica Scandinavica, 80,* 180–182.

5. Lester, D. (1990). The effects of detoxification of domestic gas on suicide in the United States. *American Journal of Public Health, 80,* 80–81.

6. Oliver, R. G., & Hetzel, B. S. (1972). Rise and fall of suicide rates in Australia: Relation to sedative availability. *Medical Journal of Australia, 2,* 919–923.

7. Yamasawa, K., Nishimukai, H., Ohbora, Y., & Inoue, S. (1980). Statistical study of suicides through intoxication. *Acta Medicinae Legalis et Socialis, 30,* 187–192.

8. Hawton, K., Simkin, S., Deeks, J., Cooper, J., Johnston, A., Waters, K., . . . & Simpson, K. (2004). UK legislation on analgesic packs: Before and after study of long term effect on poisonings. *British Medical Journal, 239,* 1076.

9. Kwon, J., Chun, H., & Cho, S. (2009). A closer look at the increase in suicide rates in South Korea from 1986-2005. *BMC Public Health, 9,* 72.

10. The article can be accessed at http://www.theatlantic.com/international/archive/2012/07/a-land-without-guns-how-japan-has-virtually-eliminated-shooting-deaths/260189/

11. http://www.sbs.com.au/news/article/2017/03/23/japan-suicide-rate-continues-drop

12. You can explore these data at http://www.gunpolicy.org/

13. Chapman, S., Alpers, P., Agho, K., & Jones, M. (2006). Australia's 1996 gun law reforms: Faster falls in firearm deaths, firearm suicides, and a decade without mass shootings. *Injury Prevention, 12,* 365–372.

14. Leigh, A., & Neill, C. (2010). Do gun buybacks save lives? Evidence from panel data. *American Law and Economics Review. doi: 10.1093/aler/ahq013*

15. http://www.mindframe-media.info/for-media/reporting-suicide/facts-and-stats

16. https://www.theguardian.com/society/2016/mar/09/highest-australian-suicide-rate-in-13-years-driven-by-men-aged-40-to-44

17. http://www.livingisforeveryone.com.au/uploads/LIFE_fact_sheet_3_final.pdf

18. I discussed this paper in an earlier chapter, but would encourage curious readers to consult Joiner et al (2016) in Psychological Review to learn more about eusociality and its relevance to suicide

19. Kaneko, Y., Yamasaki, A., & Arai, K. (2009). The Shinto religion and suicide in Japan. In D. Wasserman & C. Wasserman (Eds.), *Oxford textbook of suicidology and suicide prevention* (pp. 37–42). doi: 10.1093/med/9780198570059.001.0001

20. Wiltshire, M. G. (1983). The suicide problem in the Pali Canon. *Journal of the International Association of Buddhist Studies, 6,* 123–140.

21. Teo, A. R., & Gaw, A. C. (2010). Hikikomori, a Japanese culture-bound syndrome of social withdrawal? A proposal for DSM-5. *Journal of Nervous and Mental Disease, 198,* 444–449.

22. http://aaimedicine.org/journal-of-insurance-medicine/jim/1990/022-04-0268.pdf

23. Yim, H. (2002). Cultural identity and cultural policy in South Korea. *International Journal of Cultural Policy, 8,* 37–48.

24. http://www.npr.org/sections/parallels/2015/04/15/393939759/the-all-work-no-play-culture-of-south-korean-education

25. Khazem, L. R., & Anestis, M. D. (2016). Thinking or doing? An examination of well-established suicide risk factors within the ideation-to-action framework. *Psychiatry Research, 245,* 321–326.

26. Franklin, J. C., Ribeiro, J. D., Fox, K. R., Bentley, K. H., Kleiman, E. M., Huang, X., . . .& Nock, M. K. (2017). Risk factors for suicidal thoughts and behaviors: A meta-analysis of 50 years of research. *Psychological Bulletin, 143,* 187–232.

Conclusion

1. You can learn more about this project at https://afsp.org/nations-largest-suicide-prevention-organization-launches-suicide-prevention-firearm-pilot-program/

2. Joiner, T. E., & Stanley, I. H. (2016). Can the phenomenology of a suicidal crisis be usefully understood as a suite of antipredator defensive reactions? *Psychiatry, 79,* 107–119.

3. Kellerman, A. L., Somes, G., Rivara, F. P., Lee, R. K., & Banton, J. G. (1998). Injuries and deaths due to firearms in the home. *Journal of Trauma, 45,* 263–267.

4. Dahlberg, L. L., Ikeda, R. M., & Kresnow, M. (2004). Guns in the home and risk of a violent death in the home: Findings from a national study. *American Journal of Epidemiology, 160,* 929–936.

5. This statistic comes from an unpublished study conducted by researchers at Harvard and Northwestern that received significant international media coverage in September 2016. This information can be read at https://www.theguardian.com/us-news/2016/sep/19/us-gun-ownership-survey

About the Author

Michael D. Anestis, PhD, is a leading expert on guns and suicide. He is an associate professor of psychology at the University of Southern Mississippi. His research interests include suicide risk factors and firearms, the capacity for suicide, pain response, and emotion dysregulation. He was awarded the 2014 President's New Researcher Award from the Association for Behavioral and Cognitive Therapies and the 2015 Rising Star Award from the Association for Psychological Science.

Index

Tables and figures are indicated by an italic *t* or *f* following the page number.

mental health-care resources, utilization of, 53–54
suicide rates after detoxification of gas, 74, 74f
suicide rates by, 11–12, 12t
global gun ownership, 41t
Gooen-Piels, Jane, 72
Grafton Bridge, Auckland, New Zealand, 75–76
Green, Brad, 54
gun locks, 93–94, 96, 105
gun ownership
in Australia, 125
District of Columbia v. Heller, 83–84
Firearms Control Regulations Act, 82–83
global, 41t
in Japan, 121–122
rise in, 81
in South Korea, 122
suicide and, 33–37
in United States, 40–44, 122
GunPolicy.org, 122, 125
gun rights advocates, 113t
guns. *See also* firearm suicides; gun ownership; legislation
buying, 34
importance in suicide, 37
knowledge of, 43
lethality of, 37–40
safe drop locations for, 112
storage of, 34, 104–108
gun safes, 8, 104
Gun Safety Initiative, 112
Gun Shop Project, 110–111
Gun Violence Archive, 10–11
Guse, Clare, 88–89

health-care providers, role in means safety, 113t
Health Policy, 86
Hemenway, David, 86
Hempstead, Katherine, 86
hikikomori, 128
HIV/AIDS
lessons learned from national campaign, 70
means safety, 66–69
percent of Americans with, 47, 47f
stigma related to, 72, 73
Holland, Jimmie, 72
homicide deaths
demographics, 13t
versus suicide deaths, 9, 10f, 13, xiii
hotspots, suicide, 76

Houtsma, Claire, 36
Hyo, 129
hyperarousal, 106, 135

ideation to action framework, 31
IDF. *See* Israeli Defense Force
IDU. *See* intravenous drug use
impulsivity, 28–31
inability to predict suicide, 6
individualist cultures, 129
insight fallacy, 138
intentional overdose, 38, 39t, 58
interpersonal connections, 22–23
Interpersonal Theory of Suicide (ITS), 65
capability for suicide, 25–28
impulsivity, 28–31
path to suicidal behavior, 27f
path to suicidal thoughts, 24–25, 24f
perceived burdensomeness, 24–25
thwarted belongingness, 22–24
intravenous drug use (IDU), 67–68, 70
Israeli Defense Force (IDF), 97, 119
ITS. *See* Interpersonal Theory of Suicide

JAMA. *See Journal of the American Medical Association*
JAMA Internal Medicine, 86
Japan
cultural history of suicide, 126–127
detoxification of gas, 119
gun ownership in, 121–122
hikikomori, 128
kamikaze attacks, 126–127
seppuku, 126–127
suicide rates in, 120, 121f
suicide risk in, 128
Jefferson, Thomas, 79
Johnson, Magic, 66
Joiner, Thomas
blinking rate as sign of suicide risk, 105–106
importance of proposed solutions, 63
Interpersonal Theory of Suicide, 21–22, 25, 30
predatory threat, response to, 135
Journal of Community Health, 85
Journal of Preventative Medicine, 88–89
Journal of Psychiatric Research, 95
Journal of the American Medical Association (JAMA), 88
jumping deaths, prevention of, 75–76

Kalesan, Bindu, 41
kamikaze attacks, 126–127
Kessler, Ronald, 46
Klonsky, David, 31–32, 43, 123